CONTENTS

THE PACIFIC CREST TRAIL

CAMPO TO MANNING PARK

2650 miles

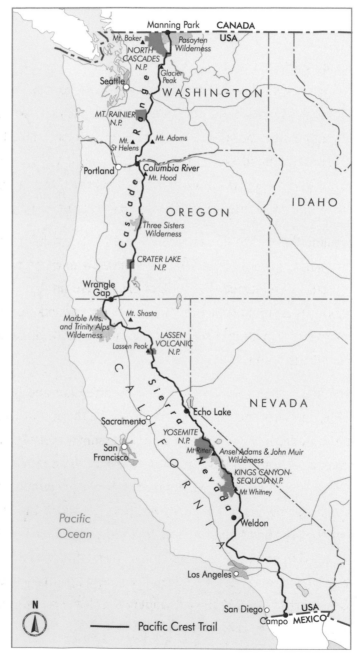

RATTLESNAKES
and BALD EAGLES
HIKING THE PACIFIC CREST TRAIL

CHRIS TOWNSEND

First published in Great Britain and the United States of America by
Sandstone Press Ltd
Dochcarty Road
Dingwall
Ross-shire
IV15 9UG
Scotland

www.sandstonepress.com

EDITOR: Robert Davidson
MAPS: David Langworth, Melrose
TECHNICAL ASSISTANCE: David Ritchie
© Chris Townsend 2014
© All photographs unless otherwise ascribed Chris Townsend 2014

The publisher acknowledges support from Creative Scotland toward publication of this volume.

ISBN: 978-1-908737-73-1

Book and cover design by Heather Macpherson of Raspberry Creative Type, Edinburgh
Printed and bound by Ozgraf, Poland

ACKNOWLEDGEMENTS

Many people helped to make my walk a success and deserve thanks. Some of their names I no longer remember after all these years (or perhaps never knew). I apologise to anyone I've omitted.

The late Warren Rogers' assistance was greatly appreciated. Without him planning the walk would have been much harder. Warren is also to be thanked for the decades of work he put in promoting the PCT. Without his efforts the trail as we know it might well not exist. Thanks to his son Don Rogers for the photos of Warren Rogers.

My companions on the trail all added to the walk, especially my companions in the High Sierra, Scott Steiner, Dave Rehbehn and Larry Lake, without whom I probably would not have made it through the snow. I certainly wouldn't have survived the river crossings in Yosemite National Park without Larry. Elsewhere on the trail I enjoyed the company of Wayne Fuiten, Ron Ellis, Ron DiBaccio, Jay J.Johnson, Greg Poirier, Susie and Robert.

Throughout the walk everyone I met was supportive and friendly (with one exception as described in the book) and many local people went out of their way to provide assistance. These trail angels included Richard in Big Bear City, Phil and Bing Le Feuvre in Wrightwood, Delree Todd in Acton, Mrs Davison in the Mohave Desert, Ralph and Betty Morgan at the Fairmont Inn, Bob Frost in Sierra City, Rene Forman in Ashland.

Outdoor clothing company Rohan provided me with most of the clothing for the walk – and with work afterwards (I took part in a series of road shows talking to people about my PCT walk and how the clothing had performed).

Thanks to Barney Mann of the Pacific Crest Trail Association for all his help. The Pacific Crest Trail Association didn't exist in 1982 but it is now an essential organisation for anything to do with the PCT and a wonderful resource which I used for much of the information on the history of the trail and the trail today.

I also discussed the PCT today with recent thru-hikers John Manning, Colin Ibbotson and Keith Foskett and learnt much about the current trail experience.

Robert Davidson of Sandstone Press suggested the book to me and encouraged and cajoled me during the writing. Heather Macpherson of Raspberry Creative Type did the design, Dave Ritchie scanned the slides, David Langworth did the maps. Thanks to them all.

My partner Denise Thorn read the manuscript and made many useful suggestions and corrections that have improved the book.

To Denise

A Note on Photography

My walk taking place long before the advent of digital photography I used Kodachrome 64 transparency film. The images in the book are scans from the transparencies.

THE PACIFIC CREST TRAIL: BEGINNINGS

Walking, camping, being in wild places. I am passionate about all three, a passion expressed in full in long distance wilderness walks, walks that take many weeks or months to complete, walks in which I can immerse myself in nature and the simple act of walking. These passions have deep roots. My love of the outdoors has been part of me as long as I can remember. Brought up in the countryside I spent my childhood exploring fields and woods. As I grew older I discovered camping and hills and wilder places. Days out became weekends, then weeks, then months. Staying out longer made trips more intense, more committing, more exciting.

No trip was totally fulfilling though, none was perfect. I didn't know what was lacking but there was always something. I suspect it was real wildness, wildness on an epic scale. Then I discovered the Pacific Crest Trail. I can still remember the thrill of excitement on first reading about it. The idea of hiking some 2,600 miles from Mexico to Canada through deserts, forests and mountains seemed both preposterous and inviting. I remember feeling a sense of both excitement and determination. I would hike this trail.

Now, over thirty years later, I look back on the PCT with affection and gratitude. It was the defining walk of my life, the walk that set the pattern for all those that followed. Successive long walks, in the USA, Canada, Scandinavia, Scotland, have sometimes been more challenging, more demanding and more remote. All have been worthwhile. None though has been like the PCT. The walks I did before the PCT became an apprenticeship, a preparation for the real thing, though at the time I didn't know what it was or even that it existed. The walks after the PCT were a continuation of the joy I had found on that trail. On the PCT I learnt how much I value trail life, wild camping, moving on every day, staying out for months at a time. I thought I knew this before the PCT but I didn't know just how deep it could go, just how much it could be an essential part of my being. After the PCT I knew it would never leave me and that I would always want to return to the trails and the wilderness.

Warren Rogers with homemade pack in 1935
© Donald Rogers

When I first read about the PCT I already knew I wanted to visit the wildernesses of the Western USA, having been inspired by first a slide show and then a book. The slide show was given in 1976 by a ranger from Yosemite National Park who was on an exchange with a ranger from the Peak District National Park in England. I marvelled at his images of vast pristine forests and huge granite mountains, all shining in brilliant sunshine, and felt overwhelmed at his stories – black bears, coyotes, real wilderness, summer-long sunshine, vast distances. How could I not want to go there? Not that I could imagine really doing so at the time. However two years later I did undertake my first really long walk, 1250 miles the length of mainland Britain from Land's End to John O'Groats on trails and cross-country, and learnt that I loved multi-week walks, especially in wild country, the Scottish Highlands being my favourite part of that walk.

At the time I was working in an outdoor store. A customer, knowing of my long walk, lent me a book he'd picked up in the USA. It was Colin Fletchers' *The Thousand-Mile Summer*, which told the story of a wilderness walk the length of California (and which I think is still one of the best long-distance walking books). I read it and was hooked. I had to do something like this. How I didn't know. I couldn't imagine trying to plan a walk in the USA from scratch (remember this was before the Internet – I'd never hiked outside Britain either). Then, browsing the outdoor section of a bookshop, I came across guidebooks to the Pacific Crest Trail. Suddenly the knowledge there was a trail with guidebooks made a long walk seem feasible, seemed a way into a very faraway wild land, a land that seemed almost mythical to me at the time. Not that the guidebooks were encouraging as they basically said doing the whole trail in one hike was a bad idea and probably not possible. That however didn't put me off. The idea of a trail stretching all the way from Mexico to Canada through the wilderness – the deserts, forests and mountains – of the western USA was just too exciting. It was a visionary idea that I felt cried out for a continuous walk.

Exactly how the bold and imaginative idea for the trail arose is somewhat clouded. It first came, it seems, from outdoorswoman and teacher Catherine Montgomery who in 1926 suggested it to Joseph Hazard, a well-known member of The Mountaineers outdoor club. He put it forward to The Mountaineers and the idea was adopted. Then, somehow, one Clinton C. Clarke became involved in the early 1930s. Often referred to as the father of the PCT it was Clarke who actually began promoting the trail, setting up the Pacific Crest Trail System Conference in 1932. This federation of hiking clubs and youth groups had the task of devising a route for the PCT. The first meeting of the Conference was held in 1935 and in 1939 the PCT first appeared on a federal government map. * Clarke also compiled the first books on the PCT. The third version of these, *The Pacific Crest Trailway*, was published in 1945 and is available online, courtesy of Daniel Craig Giffen (pcttrailway.pctplanner.com). In this book Clarke makes clear that one of the purposes of the PCT in his eyes was the preservation of the wilderness, describing it as 'the cord that binds this necklace; each gem encased in a permanent wilderness protected from all mechanization and commercialization'. He also saw the trail as character building and educational, writing 'the Pacific Crest Trailway is not a recreational project for the casual camper and hiker; it is a serious educational project for building sturdy bodies, sound minds and active, patriotic citizenship'. The words, perhaps, sound dated now but the intent is I think still true.

Although some sections of trail that would become part of the PCT were in place in the early 1930s, such as the Cascade Crest Trail in Washington, the Skyline Trail in Oregon and the John Muir Trail in California there was no route much of the way so Clarke organised a series of relays during the summers from 1935 to 1938. These consisted of groups of young outdoorsmen from the YMCA under the leadership of one Warren Rogers. By walking from Mexico to Canada the YMCA teams showed that a continuous trail was possible. A log book was kept throughout and passed on from group to group – a book I would see when I visited Warren before my hike. The 2,300 mile route described in those logs, a route devised and explored in the 1930s, is the basis for the PCT today. After the relays Rogers followed Clarke in promoting the trail, keeping the idea going for the next thirty and more years. Indeed, Rogers work and passion for the trail kept the idea alive at a time when interest in backpacking and long-distance trails was low. This changed in the 1960s and the federal government set up a committee to look at a trails system. This led to official acknowledgement in 1968 when the PCT was designated one of the first two National Scenic Trails (the other being the Appalachian Trail). Despite this designation the PCT was nowhere near complete in 1968. In fact it was to be another 25 years before the trail was officially finished (though due to its length and nature there have been and will be further changes), which meant it was far from completion for my 1982 hike.

At the same time as officialdom was working on the trail more information and support was appearing for hikers. In 1971, three years after the trail became official, Rogers had founded the Pacific Crest Trail Club to provide information and help for long distance hikers, not that many were around back then. Two years later in 1973 the first guidebooks were published by Wilderness Press, and this is where I come in as these were the guidebooks I was to find in a bookshop five years later. I wrote to the Pacific Crest Club in 1981 about my proposed hike and received a very helpful and encouraging reply from Warren Rogers.

The Pacific Crest Trail Club eventually merged with the Pacific Crest Trail System Conference in 1987 to become the Pacific Crest Trail Conference, which Rogers ran until the early 1990s. In 1992 the name was changed to the Pacific Crest Trail Association, as it still is today. In 1993 the PCTA became the federal government's official partner in managing the PCT. In the same year the trail was officially completed and a ceremony was held to mark this in Soledad Canyon in Southern California. Since then the PCTA has worked to maintain and protect the trail, describing itself as 'the voice of the PCT, its steward and its guardian'.

The trail was becoming better known, in large part due to the success of Eric Ryback's 1973 book *The High Adventure of Eric Ryback*, which told the story of his 1970 hike. This book hadn't made it across the Atlantic at the time so I didn't even know it existed. It was to be many years after my walk before I read it. At the time of Ryback's hike only three end-to-end trips had been done, according to the list maintained by the Pacific Crest Trail Association and published on their website, and those were the first on foot by Martin Papendick in 1952 and the first on horseback by Don and June Muford in 1959. Six others are listed as hiking the trail the same year as Ryback. The year after his book was published the numbers of end-to-end hikers, known as thru-hikers, reached double figures for the first time. Other noteworthy early thru-hikes were the first by a woman in 1972 – Mary Carstens, hiking with Jeff Smukler – and the first solo one by a woman in 1976, Teddi Boston. Boston's achievement is all the greater because she also started at the Canadian border, which makes the hike much harder.

Food drop schedule

By 1982, the year of my hike, 241 hikers are listed as having completed the trail. That year eleven more, including myself, were added to the list. The trail was steadily growing in popularity with numbers rising rapidly through the 1990s and 2000s. By the end of 2013 2953 hikers had completed the trail (still fewer than the number of people who have climbed Mount Everest!). With hundreds of hikers (the PCTA estimates 700-900 a year, of whom roughly 50% finish) setting off every spring the trail experience is very different now from what it was back when I hiked it, as I'll discuss later.

Warren Rogers didn't play down the difficulties but didn't say hiking the whole trail was impossible either. I also came across two books that greatly encouraged me as they were by thru-hikers. David Green's *A Pacific Crest Odyssey*, which told the story of his 1977 thru-hike, and Chuck Long's *Pacific Crest Trail Hike Planning Guide*, which included information from 15 hikers,

Guidebook pages.

including Long himself, who had hiked all or most of the trail, were devoured many times in the months and years before my walk as I tried to absorb something of the reality of what would be involved.

Overall four years elapsed from finding out about the trail – and knowing immediately I wanted to hike it – and setting out from the Mexican border. During those years there were periods of intense planning and periods of suspense and waiting. There was also the question of money. I didn't know how much such a walk would cost but I knew I'd need to have money put aside for it and this would take time. Planning such a long walk through such wild country was not easy even with the existence of a trail, guidebooks and the Pacific Crest Club. This was my first big backpacking trip outside Britain – my only other one was a two-week trip in the Pyrenees, undertaken as part of my preparation for the PCT as I wanted to experience higher altitudes than those found in Britain before I set out (I climbed the highest mountain, 11,168 foot Pico d'Aneto). The PCT was also over twice as long as my Land's End to John O'Groats walk and in much remoter and wilder country. For making the planning much easier than it would have been without his help I have to thank Warren Rogers. He advised me, checked my plans and sent me information. As well as reading all I could about the trail I made and revised lists of gear and compiled lists of supplies and the post offices to which they would be sent. I also ripped up the Wilderness Press guidebooks into sections to go in my supply packages. Warren produced basic strip maps for the Pacific Crest Club and offered to send me these in batches every few hundred miles. I also planned on buying topographic maps when I reached the USA. Warren said I wouldn't need these but being used to Britain's detailed Ordnance Survey maps I knew I'd feel ill-equipped without what I thought of as proper maps.

So what is special about the Pacific Crest Trail, other than the distance? What called me across the ocean and across a continent to walk for nearly six months carrying everything on my back? The simple answer is nature and a wild landscape on a monumental scale, a scale hard to imagine for a walker from Britain. The PCT follows the westernmost chains of mountains in the USA and is in wilderness or near-wilderness for virtually the whole of its 2650 miles. Despite the name it's not that close to the Pacific Ocean and there is no sense of the sea as a wide plain lies west of the mountains. What the PCT does have, which seemed strange and exotic to me, is a taste of the desert. More than a taste in the first 500 miles in fact. This desert feel fades as the trail progresses north until the climate is more akin to that of Britain, as I was to find out.

For roughly the first 500 miles from the Mexican border the PCT changes character frequently as it climbs from desert and chaparral to forested mountains and back again time after time. The mountain ranges here are fairly small in area but still rise to over 11,000 feet. They're known as the transverse ranges as they tend to run east-west rather than north-south. This means a great deal of ascent and descent as the PCT crosses each one. Real desert is encountered at the end of this section when the Mohave Desert is crossed before the PCT reaches the southern end of the Sierra Nevada mountains, which it follows for around 1000 miles.

The southern Sierra Nevada – the High Sierra – is the highest section of the PCT, with the trail lying above 10,000 feet for many miles and reaching 13,153 feet on Forester Pass. This is a granite wonderland with magnificent peaks rising above tremendous forests. Here the PCT follows the John Muir Trail much of the way and passes through King Canyons-Sequoia and Yosemite National Parks. North of Yosemite the Sierra Nevada slowly becomes less dramatic and the mountains are lower, though this is still fine country. Unnoticeable to the walker the Sierra Nevada merges with the southern Cascade Range which the PCT then follows all the way to Canada. The Cascade Range is characterised by big volcanic peaks towering over the lower hills and forests, the first of which is met in Northern California with Lassen Peak in Lassen Volcanic National Park. Through Oregon the PCT is at its gentlest, winding past the mountains through forests and meadows before descending to the Columbia River and the trail's low point of 140 feet. There follows a long thrilling finale to the PCT as it climbs into the rugged and spectacular mountains of Washington State, culminating in the grandeur of the North Cascades. In total the PCT passes through six national parks and forty-eight designated wilderness areas, which shows the value placed on the landscape and the natural history of the trail's environs.

Finally my planning, or at least the British part of it, was over and I boarded an aircraft for the first time ever for the long flight to Los Angeles with instructions from Warren Rogers to catch a bus from the airport to Disneyland, where he would meet me. Very kindly he had invited me to stay with him and his wife Mary for a couple of days. Standing outside Disneyland in the dark dazed from the long flight I remember feeling a little unsure and a long way from home. A tall man strode over and shook my hand firmly. It was Warren. I guess my large pack and air of bewilderment made identifying me easy.

Warren's enthusiasm for the PCT came over immediately. I knew his feelings from his letters but hearing him speak really impressed upon me how important the trail was for him. Advice and suggestions tumbled out. He showed me the precious log book from the 1930s relays, kept safely in a fireproof box. I felt I was looking at a holy relic.

One important task remained before I could start the walk. I needed to sort out food supplies. Warren reckoned I could probably find suitable breakfast foods and trail snacks along the way but that evening meals would be a problem. However he knew of a company that would send food parcels to post offices along the way so on my first full day in the USA he drove me out to North Hollywood to meet Charlie Yacoobin of Trail Foods. Here I selected what I hoped would prove adequate and tasty from a bewildering array of freeze-dried and dehydrated food. Being vegetarian I was pleased to find quite a choice of suitable food – I wouldn't be living on macaroni and cheese for six months (a hiker's staple that I was to eat rather too often on subsequent walks). This wasn't the cheapest way to buy food but bringing six months' worth from Britain was not an option and I didn't have the time to visit supermarkets, buy food and repackage it – my visa for the USA was for six months, the longest period available, and I knew it might take that long to complete the trail. Most of the food was for evening meals but I stuck some snacks and breakfast food into the twenty-six parcels just in case I needed it plus the relevant sections of the guidebook and some rolls of film (this was long before digital photography) and left Charlie with the list of post offices.

So far all I'd seen of the USA was Disneyland, miles of low buildings, heavy traffic and freeways. The air was hot and heavy, the horizons hazy and faint. There was no sense of wild country and not much of nature. That was soon to change. I'd planned on catching buses to San Diego and then Campo at the start of the trail, a two-day trip. Warren vetoed that

From the left Warren Rogers' son Paul, Warren Rogers and Merritt Podley © Donald Rogers

idea and said he'd drive me, saving a day and giving me more time to hear his stories of the trail. As we sped down the highway the hot arid scenery of Southern California flashed past the windows. I couldn't relate to it yet, couldn't feel it as real, didn't know what it felt like. I would soon learn.

Warren dropped me at a campground in the tiny border hamlet of Campo, wished me luck and left me standing by the pack I was to live out of for half a year. I waved as he drove away. Alone in the dusk I realised the adventure was about to begin. High above the familiar constellation of Orion hung in the clear sky and there was bright half-moon. All the planning and preparation was over. All that was left was to walk to Canada.

* See these two pdf documents for more information on the founding of the PCT and also the fascinating research of Barney "Scout" Mann of the Pacific Crest Trail Association who investigated Catherine Montgomery and Clinton C. Clarke. http://www.pcta.org/wp-content/uploads/2012/10/Montgomery_March11.pdf. http://www.pcta.org/wp-content/uploads/2012/10/Clarke_Dec10_spreads.pdf.

CHAPTER 1

DESERTS & SNOW:
SOUTHERN CALIFORNIA

CAMPO TO WELDON
April 3 to May 9
513 miles

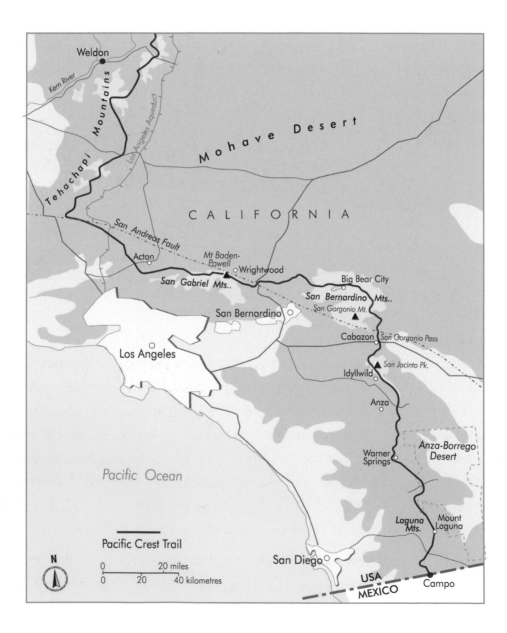

A broken-down barbed wire fence by a dirt road in nondescript desert scrub marked the border with Mexico. There were no notices, no signs, nothing to indicate the start of the PCT (there's a monument now). I didn't mind. I felt happy to be there alone and happy there was no signpost saying 'Canada, 2650 miles'. This was my journey and I suddenly felt very possessive of it. For this year the PCT was my personal and private trail, no matter how many others I met along the way. Starting alone gave me the chance to absorb these early feelings and relish the beginning of a great adventure.

I took a few self-portraits, the camera balanced on a rock, then turned away from the border and took my first steps northwards. The journey really had begun. I felt a little unreal, elated yet calm. I didn't know what to think about what lay ahead.

At the Mexican border

The landscape here wasn't spectacular or even particularly wild. Locals probably wouldn't give it a second glance. For me it was quite unusual though, a semi-desert environment totally unlike anywhere in Britain. A sparse scrub of tough, drought-resistant bushes covered the ground, interspersed with small cacti and clumps of rough-barked Live Oak trees. Lizards and ground squirrels darted over the ground. This was the chaparral, vegetation I was to become very familiar with over the next few weeks. I thought it superb. The route led along dirt roads past a few ranches then after a few miles the PCT became a footpath. And I promptly lost it! I was heading in the right direction though and soon picked it up again.

After 14 miles I reached the campground where I planned on stopping for the night. To my surprise it had no water. I'd never heard of a campground without water before. I had none left either and was thirsty, having set off with far less than I needed. I hadn't really registered that early April this far south would be so hot or that there would be little water on the trail. I quickly learnt that I must carry plenty of water. And know where the next water was to be found and drink deeply from every source. This was desert hiking and heat and thirst were major hazards. Luckily for me this first evening there was a campground host and she kindly gave me some water. This was the first example of a 'trail angel', a term I hadn't heard yet but which was to become familiar. Trail angels are people who help hikers, often going out of their way to do so, and one of the aspects of trail life that gives faith in the essential goodness of humanity. The host's son, a local volunteer ranger, gave me some tips about the next few days hiking, including possible water sources. I was on my way.

My pack and the first of many trail signs

That first day my feet had become very sore and swollen in my heavy leather boots, another hazard of desert hiking. I'd removed the insoles to allow them more room but they still ached. My arms and neck were sunburnt too, despite applying sunscreen liberally several times. Time for my sunhat, I thought the next day. The sun really was the dominant feature of the first few days on the trail; hot, white and relentless. There was little shade and few shadows. Just blazing light. The sky was vast in this flat landscape, the horizons far distant. Used to the rapidly changing scenery and landscape of the British hills I felt at times as though I was walking on the spot. Only the movement of the sun showed the progression of time.

On day two I walked mostly on wide sandy and gravelly trails through the dense, often shoulder-height, impenetrable chaparral.

Towards the end of the day the first hills appeared; the Laguna Mountains. The trail climbed upwards beside big red rock boulders. In the shade of one of these I met my first other PCT hikers, Scott and Jim, sitting next to huge packs with gear strapped all over the outside that looked frighteningly heavy. I gazed at them wonderingly. Was I under-equipped? I was relieved when they told me this was their third day out and the weight of their packs was already a problem. I never saw them again or heard how much further they hiked. The PCTA says only 50% of thru hikers actually complete the trail today. Back in 1982 with far less information available, and heavier gear, the percentage was lower. At least 120 through-permits were issued by the Forest Service in 1982. Only eleven of us completed a through-hike to Canada. Of the others some dropped out completely while some skipped snowbound sections and only did part of the trail.

The Laguna Mountains only reach a little over 6,000 feet, small in Western U.S. terms, but are still high enough to have a different environment to the desert not far below (and still more than 1500 feet higher than the highest mountain in Britain but then the PCT at the Mexican border is nearly 3,000 feet high). As I climbed into the Lagunas the chaparral gave way to sparse oak woods and then denser pine forest, my first experience of the wonderful pine forests I was to revel in all the way to Canada. Out to the east I could see the lifeless orange void of the Anza-Borrego Desert shimmering in a heat haze. The rich, reddish-barked pines gave welcome shade under their spreading boughs. These were Jeffery pines, the commonest conifers in Southern California as they are extremely drought resistant. Growing between 5000 and 9000 feet they cloak the mountains that rise out of the desert.

The change as I entered the pine forest was abrupt and dramatic. Here it was cool and humid with moist air rising from the snow patches that dotted the ground between the widely spaced trees. Someone had even been skiing here, their parallel tracks following the line of the trail. I found this unusual as I hadn't discovered cross-country skiing at the time – later in the walk I was to travel with two skiers and realise how useful skis were for crossing deep snow. I'd meet this skier in a week's time but for now I was alone. I camped beside a little creek in the forest, the first wild camp of the walk. I wasn't far from a road though and a little exploration revealed a Mexican restaurant. I'd already learnt on my British long walks that passing by any opportunity for food was unwise so I forgot the instant noodles and packet soup I'd brought from home for these first few days and dined on much more appetising tortillas and enchiladas.

Notebooks

Two days and twenty-eight miles into the walk and my feet were already in tatters. I had four blisters, many sore spots and they were badly swollen and ached all over. I knew I wouldn't get much further without doing something about this. I'd brought some light running shoes for town and camp wear so on day three I hiked in these. The difference was astounding. My feet felt fine again. The boots went in the pack and were to be carried many miles over the coming weeks. They were much more comfortable on my back than on my feet and proved to my satisfaction the old adage that a pound on the feet is equivalent to five pounds on the back. I could have dispensed with them altogether but I knew that much bigger mountains lay ahead where there was likely to be much more snow than these thin patches.

Early the next morning I reached my first supply point, the tiny little mountain hamlet of Mount Laguna. After collecting my supply parcel from the Post Office I called in at the little store, my journal in hand, open at the page with the first of many shopping lists that were to decorate its pages. This list read:

Pot scourer	1lb. sugar
Loo paper	1 pkt.soup
Toothpaste	Trail mix
Candles	Dried fruit
7 choc.bars	Instant breakfast
Biscuits	Jam/honey
Margarine	Postcards
Band Aids	Vit.pills

View from the Desert Divide Trail to the Anza-Borrego Desert

Eight items were checked, eight would have to wait until the next store in, I hoped, five days' time. I also marked my supply parcel list with the day of arrival, a day earlier than my estimate. Doing so brought home to me that the walk really had begun. Twenty-five parcels to go.

Mount Laguna was a secretive little place. The dark brown, low wooden houses and wide, dusty roads blended into the surrounding forest, a forest that the town had not quite escaped from, so that the buildings seemed to be hiding cautiously amongst the trees. It vanished within minutes of my heading back to my trail. All I could see behind me were the pines.

The Laguna Mountains are a tilted block of granite with the steep slope to the east. The PCT followed the crest on a path marked as the Desert Divide Trail which gave striking views down

15

to the ridged badlands of the Anza-Borrego Desert, some 4,000 feet below. A sterile brown colour, the hills in the desert came to life at dawn and dusk when they caught the rays of the setting and rising sun and glowed red and gold. Then Oriflamme Mountain was aptly named. To the west the mountains dipped slowly away into rolling pine and oak forest that in turn changed abruptly to the undulating chaparral country. Ahead lay the next mountain range, the San Jacinto Mountains, with 10,834 foot San Jacinto Peak looking very white. I would be there within a week.

A storm is approaching, I'd been told in Mount Laguna. By early afternoon flat saucer-shaped clouds indicated high winds. Soon the first cold gusts arrived and for the first time I needed to wear my warm fibre-pile jacket and balaclava. Clouds piled in on the wind but broke up as they reached the crest. There was no rain but snowmelt meant there were dozens of seasonal streams so I didn't need to carry any water. The wind and the streams continued the next day during which I descended back to the chaparral and passed boarded up old gold mines outside the tiny hamlet of Banner before road walking across the San Felipe Ranch and along a highway to San Felipe itself, another small hamlet. Here the next trail angel appeared. There was a combined gas station/sandwich store/caravan site called The Log Cabin. It was closed but as I'd run out of water I knocked on the door to ask for some. The owner appeared, welcomed me in and gave me tea and a piece of her birthday cake. Friends there to celebrate with her told me there were record snows in the Sierra Nevada, something I was to hear regularly over the next few weeks. I was given the key to an outside water tap and allowed to camp behind the building sheltered from the still strong wind.

Three more mostly uneventful and not very inspiring days on rock-hard dirt roads through flat verdant cattle country took me to the edge of the San Jacinto Mountains and the welcome shade of wooded canyons. More interesting than the walking was my first encounter with the annual gathering of 'trailers', as PCT thru-hikers were then known. Warner Springs was yet another place consisting of just a few houses – something I was already becoming used to and which was typical of towns along the PCT all the way to Canada. Here I met Joel and Jeannie sprawled in front of the post office with their dog, Riley. They'd set off two days before me and were footsore and weary. Soon two other PCT hikers arrived. They were from Finland so I wasn't the only European on the trail. Over the next few weeks I would regularly meet and hear of other trailers struggling northwards from Mexico until it felt as though a small community was on the move. Key contact points were post offices and restaurants, both essential to the wellbeing of hikers. Most post offices had PCT registers where you could check who'd already been through and look for messages and hints of what lay ahead. As this was long before the days of text messages, emails and online journals the registers were one of the few ways of finding out about other hikers and leaving messages. Some hikers also left notes along the trail both for individuals and giving general advice. Often though weeks would go by with no idea what

Chaparral country

was happening with people I'd met. Some of them I never heard about again.

Two topics dominated the register at Warner Springs: the state of people's feet and the state of the snow in the mountains to come. Rumours were spreading of the deep, late snow in the Sierra Nevada and there were stories of avalanches and even deaths (the last referred to a huge avalanche that killed seven people at the Alpine Meadows ski resort though I didn't find out about this until years later). Today of course finding out information about snow in the mountains is easy – though that wouldn't allay concerns.

None of the four hikers at Warner Springs had any snow gear – I was carrying an ice axe – and they were all concerned about the snow ahead. A phone call was made to the San Jacinto Ranger Station. There's about ten feet of snow above six thousand feet but it's quite firm, we were told. In Anza, just a few hours walk from the San Jacintos, there was a note in the PCT

17

Arriving in Anza Valley

register advising a different route down from the mountains if the snow was deep. I had more immediate problems. My second supply parcel hadn't arrived (the only one that didn't on the whole walk). The local store provided instant noodles, packet soups and boxes of macaroni and cheese sauce (mac n'cheese – a hiker staple). It would have to do. A road walk led to the start of the climb into the mountains and the snow. I read a paperback along this rather dull stretch of walking, something that was to become a habit on this and future long walks.

Not far beyond a last cafe, which provided coffee and sandwiches (I already knew never to pass one by, it could be the last for a long time) I entered the San Bernardino National Forest and camped amongst the pines. I'd been out a week and had walked 115 miles. The going had been easy other than the heat but there'd been rather too many roads. I was looking forward to bigger mountains and wilder terrain.

As if to welcome me to the mountains and remind me I'd left the desert light rain fell during the evening, the first of the walk. The morning dawned sunny though and I set off in shorts, enjoying the views. There were a few patches of soft snow but nothing to impede progress. Then out of nowhere came a furious storm. Within minutes I was being lashed by wind-driven rain. The visibility dropped to less than ten yards. The first real mountains of the walk had brought the first real mountain weather. As I climbed the snow grew deeper. The firm surface the ranger had mentioned had gone, softened by the rain and the sun. Soon I was slogging through two-feet deep snow, raising each leg high then plunging it back down into the snow, an arduous and slow method of progress that I was to learn is known as post-holing. My lower legs and feet were soaked by the snow and soon felt very cold as I didn't have any gaiters. As the terrain steepened I used my ice axe for balance and security. It had seemed incongruous in the desert. I was glad of it now. I lost the line of the trail in the deep snow but pushed on in roughly the right direction, using my compass for the first time. Eventually the rain stopped but the wind and mist continued with gusts lifting the edge of the clouds occasionally to give unreal glimpses 7,000 feet down to the desert floor where the city of Palm Springs basked in bright sunlight.

Suddenly a bright red tent loomed up in the gloom. The four hikers inside told me they'd turned back due to the storm and the deep snow. They were just out for a few days but told me that three PCT hikers weren't far ahead. I wouldn't meet those hikers for a while but they were to prove very important for my walk. I pushed on into the storm but soon decided to camp. Going on seemed pointless as I wasn't sure where I was or how severe conditions might become. Trees gave shelter from the wind and the snow provided water, melted over my little gasoline stove. I considered my options and decided that if the storm or the snow worsened I would have to descend west to the town of Idyllwild and go round the rest of the San Jacintos at a lower level. Despite the storm and the hard going and the uncertainty I felt elated. It had been an exciting mountain day. Now I hoped for the temperature to drop enough overnight to harden the snow.

I woke to thick mist, strong winds and a temperature of +8°C (47°F). The snow was even softer than the day before. After an hour of great effort and little progress I decided retreat was sensible. The terrain was steepening, balls of snow were sliding down the slopes around me and navigation was difficult. The reward for my prudence was a second breakfast of blueberry cobbler and coffee with the four campers in the red tent. Continuing down I reached a road and was soon in the pleasant mountain resort of Idyllwild. The rain was still pouring down. At the ranger station I learnt that the PCT down the San Jacintos wasn't complete and the Forest Service advised taking the road through Idyllwild anyway.

On the campground I discovered five other PCT hikers who'd all walked the road from Anza to avoid the snow. Joel and Jeannie I'd met before. New were another couple, Ron and Cheryl, and a solo hiker named Ken, whose ski tracks I'd seen in the Laguna Mountains. Inevitably discussion turned to the snow in the Sierra Nevada. I hadn't considered not going through, snow or no snow, despite my experience in the San Jacintos. Only Ken was of like mind. The others were all going to road walk until the snow thawed. Various birds fluttered round the campground. The others identified them for me – bright blue beautiful but raucous Stellar's jays and red-capped black and white acorn woodpeckers, which hammered acorns into holes in trees as food stores. I'd noticed a pine riddled with acorns and had wondered how they'd got there. I'd also seen both birds before but not known what they were. I added a natural history guide to my shopping list.

Acorn Woodpeckers food store

I'd now been out ten days, of which the last two had been tough, so I decided to have a rest day in Idyllwild and hope that the storm would fade. I also needed to see a dentist, having cracked a couple of fillings. The last meant a second day in Idyllwild as I couldn't get an appointment until the next afternoon. The rest would probably be beneficial, I decided, though I quickly felt very restless even though Idyllwild, set amongst magnificent tall trees and with towering rock peaks rising high above, was a good place for a stop. The town offered facilities I hadn't seen elsewhere too, which I undoubtedly needed, namely showers and a laundromat.

A two-day road walk led down through the wooded foothills of the San Jacintos to Cabazon and the San Gorgonio Pass, a tongue of desert protruding into the mountains between the massive 10,000 foot walls of San Jacinto Peak and Mount San Gorgonio. Wandering round Cabazon I encountered three battered, weatherworn and somewhat haggard figures walking towards me. They could only be PCT hikers and so it turned out. Scott Steiner, Dave Rehbehn and Larry Lake had battled the storm in the San Jacintos while I'd been in Idyllwild, at times totally lost and once only making three miles in a whole day. But they had snowshoes, crampons and gaiters and so were better equipped for the snow than me. Finally they'd bushwhacked down to Cabazon through steep, spiny chaparral that left them scratched and scarred.

The five other hikers from Idyllwild arrived and we all crammed onto a small patch of grass behind the fire station with sprinklers all around us as there was no campground in Cabazon. I was relieved that my supplies had reached the post office and delighted to find a store selling a huge variety of dried fruit. Most of my food was pretty stodgy so a substitute for fresh fruit was welcome and I stocked up on dried figs, dates, bananas, apples and those strips of mixed dried fruit known as fruit leathers. My plan was to reach the next town, Big Bear City, in five days but I knew it might take longer in the snow so I wanted extra supplies. Dried fruit was much healthier than more candy bars, the only alternative, though I did buy some of the latter as well. The evening

was spent in a rather sleazy pizza and beer parlour (just right for scruffy hikers!) where, over several pitchers of beer, we discussed future plans and struck a deal. Scott, Dave and Larry were intending on going through the Sierra in the snow and I was pleased when they invited me to join them. I knew that being in a group would be safer and also make it

Dinosaurs in Cabazon

more likely that I would succeed in getting through the snow. The others intended to hitch-hike round the Sierra or, in Ken's case, hike the road in Owen's Valley below the mountains.

Before leaving Cabazon I needed stove fuel, as did the others. But nowhere sold the refined white gas we'd all been using. Risking death and arrest we crossed the Interstate 10 freeway to a massive gas station. One of the giant dinosaur sculptures that make Cabazon noteworthy reared overhead. In the gas station we filled our little half litre fuel bottles from the high pressure pumps. Gasoline sprayed everywhere but eventually the bottles were full. Luckily the attendant thought it was hilarious. Back in 1982 gasoline stoves were the standard for long-distance backpacking, partly because of reliability and partly because of fuel availability. Today they are rare. Now ultralight stoves running on alcohol, solid fuel tablets or butane/propane canisters are used by almost every hiker, including myself. There were few of these available back then though and fuel was hard to find.

Having completed 150 miles I felt that the first part of the journey was over. This breaking-in stage was when I became used to the life of a hiker and shed worries about food, route finding, equipment and other factors that could detract from my enjoyment of the PCT. I no longer felt like a novice on the trail and I no longer looked like one either! My face and arms were brown from the

sun, my legs were muscled and hard. My equipment, so shiny and pristine at the start, already looked quite battered and worn. I was also revelling in the adventure and loving the life of a hiker.

Ahead lay the wooded slopes of the San Bernardino and San Gabriel Mountains and beyond them the arid wastes of the Mohave

Cactus flowers

Clockwise: Bivouac under a Canyon Live Oak tree
On the trail in the San Bernardino Mountains
Scott on the trail in the San Bernardino Mountains

Desert. First though came half a day's road walking in searing heat. Cabazon, at 1400 feet, was the lowest point on the trail yet and this was a walk in real desert. I was soaked in sweat and felt exhausted after eleven miles. Interest to the trudge was provided by the first cacti in bloom I'd seen, with lovely purple flowers, and, to the south, the steep, snowy and impressive north face of San Jacinto Peak towering into the sky. I wanted to be away from roads and back in the wilds though. Leaving the unbelievably noisy, smelly and hot San Gorgonio Pass, threaded as it is by both Interstate 10 and the Southern Pacific Railroad, was a relief. I climbed thankfully into the hills beside the dirt-filled, grey rushing waters of Whitewater Creek. I met up with Scott, Dave

23

Ten Thousand Foot Ridge in the San Bernardino Mountains

and Larry again and we camped in the shade of a canyon live oak tree. For the first time I didn't bother with the tent and lay outside in my sleeping bag watching the last light of the day fading on the red and orange strata of the canyon walls.

For the next three days I hiked with my three prospective Sierra companions and we began to get to know each other. Larry had also set out on his own but had met the others within a few days of leaving the Mexican border and had travelled with them ever since. Like Scott he was a veteran of the 2,000 mile Appalachian Trail in the Eastern USA while Dave was on his first long backpacking trip. Although this was their country they were still 4,000 miles from home as they were all from eastern states (Maryland and New Jersey) and on their first visit to the West. This distance from home gave us something in common as most of the other PCT hikers we met were close enough to home to return there for a rest or to wait for the snow to melt. None of us had that option.

The climb up into the San Bernardino Mountains was difficult and frustrating as it mostly followed a flood-swept, boulder-strewn canyon in which we kept losing the trail and having to crash through dense undergrowth as well as ford Mission Creek many times. It was very hard and hot work. However there were many flowers and trees and in my journal I wrote 'more fun than the road'. The reward for our efforts came the next day when we left the canyon for a magnificent forest of pine and fir and superb views of the surrounding mountains. Deep snow drifts covered the trail in places but these were never extensive enough to impede our progress much. Our camp in the woods was at 7900 feet, the highest yet. The night was cold and, sleeping under the stars again, I woke to frost coating my sleeping bag for the first time. Our leather boots, wet from the previous days postholing, were frozen hard. The morning sun was hot though and soon thawed them out. Pleasant forest walking led down to Big Bear City, the next resupply point. Although only a small town, despite the name, with a population of around 12,000 it seemed huge to me. I was already unused to traffic and people and an urban setting. In British terms it was small for somewhere called a city but I was soon to learn that in the USA much smaller places that would be villages at home could be called cities. Although Big Bear City is a tourist town with two ski resorts nearby there was no campground. However Scott chatted to a man curious about our appearance and big packs and when he found what we were doing he said we could camp on his front lawn. Richard also drove us to a restaurant for a huge meal and then entertained us with beer and blues rock in his house. More trail magic!

One problem in town stops was that I had little in the way of spare clothing to wear and my trail clothes were usually in dire need of washing. Often I sat in a laundromat wearing nothing but my waterproof trousers while my clothes were being washed. Luckily, although much of my gear was what would now be called traditional or old-fashioned, my clothing was modern and wouldn't look out of place on the PCT today. This meant it was lightweight and fast drying. Only a few years before the walk I'd been wearing woollen trousers, shirts and sweaters and cotton windproof jackets. These garments were heavy, absorbent, slow-drying and hard to clean. However shortly before my walk a new clothing company, Rohan, had launched a range of thin, light, polyester-cotton mix clothing that was windproof, breathable, fast drying and very comfortable. I thought the clothing looked ideal for backpacking and Paul and Sarah Howcroft of Rohan kindly offered to supply me with a full set – shorts, trousers, windshirt – plus synthetic base layers. They even made me up experimental waterproof garments from a very light version

In the San Bernardino Mountains

of the then still new fabric Gore-Tex. All this clothing was easy to wash and dried very quickly so I spent less time in laundromats than I would otherwise have done. When there was water available I could also rinse garments out along the trail too and know they would dry fast. Overall the Rohan clothing was a great success, especially the polyester-cotton garments, and I never went back to the heavy wool and cotton stuff. Now of course such lightweight clothing is standard wear for hiking.

In every town I also had to buy soap powder, shampoo and other items I didn't want to carry with me. Food supplies were often only available in larger amounts than I needed too. Today I would use a bounce box but this idea hadn't been dreamed up back then. Now using one is common practice amongst thru-hikers. A bounce box is a box that is posted on from post office to post office. It can contain clothes for town wear, maps, unneeded gear, surplus supplies and more. It's a simple but brilliant concept. I wish I'd thought of it in 1982. Also common today are hiker boxes in trail towns and resorts. These contain surplus gear and supplies left by hikers for other hikers to use if needed. My surplus town items would have gone in these if they'd existed.

My companions were having a rest day in Big Bear City as their next supply point was a long ten days away. Mine was in five days so I went on. I was also quite happy to be on my own again. I'd enjoyed being with the others but conversation and companionship, although pleasant, distracted from the subtle beauty of the landscape and intruded into the silence and into my

Steep snow in the San Bernardino Mountains

feeling of contact with nature. Alone again my attention returned to the landscape and the wildlife. After more forest walking on snow and another camp in the woods I began a slow farewell to the San Bernardino Mountains as I descended beside Holcomb Creek. Once out of the snow the trail wound in and out of large sandy boulders, chaparral and scattered Jeffrey pines. The weather was hot but the snow-fed creek was cold as I found during three knee-deep fords. Camping on a deserted campground beneath big pines I lit a camp fire for the first time and sat watching the flickering flames and the dark starry sky. Suddenly I felt very self-contained and very remote, huddled by my pathetically tiny orange spot of warmth with all around the vast dark wilderness. A sense of euphoria at being alone in the natural world I had come to seek swept over me. This was perfect!

The San Bernardino Mountains

Deep Creek followed Holcomb Creek and these desert rivers, golden brown in the sunlight and black with pools and white with rapids, led enticingly on to the snowy San Gabriel Mountains, edged by the endless flatness of the Mohave Desert. Down on the desert floor there were roads and people – day hikers, anglers and car campers. The banks of the creek were awash with flowers – purple, blue, yellow and white. A great swathe of bright colours in an area my guidebook described as barren. Camped on a roadside campground I experienced the first mosquitoes of the trip though they faded away as the temperature dropped. For the first time I still felt hungry after my evening meal. I'd been out for three weeks and had already lost a great deal of weight. The food I'd chosen back at Trail Foods, which already seemed another world, was mostly okay, though there were a few meals I hoped didn't turn up often, but was going to need supplementing from now on.

The PCT became rather fractured now as it linked too many miles of paved roads with stretches of dirt road and bits of trail as I approached the great gash of the Cajon Pass, which separates the San Bernardino and San Gabriel Mountains. The convoluted sedimentary rocks around the pass formed deep tortuous canyons with names like Little Horsethief and hot, barren desert hills like Cleghorn Mountain. Unstable, narrow, alluvial arêtes of soft sand slopes set at impossible angles dominated the sides of the pass, which lies on the notorious San Andreas Fault, one of the world's major earthquake zones. This tongue of the Mohave Desert is hot and arid and the walking was enervating. Roads and railways and power lines threaded the pass. I found a pleasant enough site by a flowing creek in Crowder Canyon but I could hear traffic and trains and the crackle of the power lines. Although down in the desert it was the coldest night of the walk so far and I woke to a thick white frost coating my sleeping bag and my gear, which I'd foolishly left strewn around. Again though the sun soon dried everything. I was still surprised at how fast it heated the world and how quickly it was high in the sky. I was used to the long dawns of home, far to the north of here.

The PCT crossed Cajon Pass in a rather ignominious fashion, passing under the freeway and two railway lines via slogan-sprayed concrete culverts. Above the freeway tunnel I could hear the high-speed traffic screaming past. This was a long way from wilderness. Finally I waited at yet another railroad while a mile-long goods train slowly negotiated a steep curve. Once across the tracks I started my ascent out of the pass, the trail climbing above the pale desert sandstone sentinels of the Mormon Rocks, named by the Mormon pioneers who were some of the first white settlers to come through the pass en route for Salt Lake City in 1851. There followed a long strenuous haul up and along Upper Lyttle Creek Ridge – 'hot, waterless, shadeless & never-ending' I wrote in my journal. The ascent was made worse by latter day manifestations of the pioneer spirit as for much of the way I appeared to be in the middle of a gunfight. From each little side canyon came the cracks and echoes of small arms fire as weekend gunmen practised their skills. All the PCT signs in the area were peppered with bullet holes. Finally after 3,500 feet of climbing I reached the welcome shade of the first pines and the first snow. Soon the gunshots faded along with the desert. Camp was amongst pines and mountain mahogany bushes and again I had to

Flowers lining the trail in the desert
Overleaf: Deep Creek

Mormon Rocks and the Southern Pacific Railroad

melt snow for water. I was back in the mountains. Birds sang in the trees, a ground squirrel scampered past the tent. A squat, armoured, prehistoric-looking small lizard crawled across the ground.

A long traverse followed, on the firm snow of Blue Ridge. There were views of mountains all around – Dawson Peak, Pine Mountain, very snowy Mount Baden-Powell, the white mass of 10,064 foot Mount San Antonio, highest in the San Gabriels. West the air was hazy with smog that was insidiously creeping up the mountains from the ever closer Los Angeles basin, a poisonous brew of automobile fumes that was to be an unpleasant presence over the next few weeks as I passed the huge sprawling city.

The little town of Wrightwood was just three miles from the PCT, which is why I'd decided to use it as a supply point, preferring to walk the extra six miles in and out than carry ten days food in one go. What I didn't know was that the descent from Blue Ridge was very steep. There was supposed to be a trail but I couldn't find it in the snow and ended up descending what was probably the wrong canyon. The terrain was treacherous and the steepness unnerving. This descent was the scariest part of the walk so far. Initially I was on hard icy snow where I wished I'd had crampons and was very glad of my ice axe. This changed lower down to equally steep soft and loose snow mixed in with steep loose scree and steep loose mud. At every step the ground slipped from under me. Very scared I slithered and skidded down 3,000 feet of this, hanging off my ice axe. Finally the slope eased off and I could walk normally. Soon I was in Wrightwood, another pleasant town in the woods, where I discovered the clocks had gone forward the night before so there would be an extra hour of daylight in the evening. On the trail this didn't really matter as I didn't walk to the clock anyway. I'm not one of those hikers who's walking within minutes of waking up and who does most of the day's distance before noon (I have read that this is the mark of a serious walker). I struggle to be walking an hour after waking up. Mostly I don't even try for an early start and just wake up slowly and set off when I'm relaxed and ready then walk into the evening. I don't try and follow a set pattern either. I prefer to follow how I feel at the time and to react to my surroundings. Of course I had to plan supplies but whilst I might know that it was 90 miles to the next supply point and that I had to be there in 6 days if I wasn't to run out of food that didn't mean that I set out to walk 15 miles every day. I might walk 10 miles one day and 20 the next. I might stop to camp at a lovely site early in the afternoon or I might walk on into the night because I felt energetic. I didn't plan breaks either, unlike some walkers who like to stop for ten minutes every hour or always have an hours break half way through the day. I stopped when I felt like it, often because there was a good view or a water source, and sometimes walked for many hours without a break. Where knowing the time did matter was so that I could arrive in places before the post office closed.

As I'd arrived in Wrightwood on a Sunday I couldn't pick up my supply parcel until the next day. While I waited I went shopping for extra food, film and books so I could leave reasonably early the following morning. Remembering how hungry I'd been feeling I made up some very rich trail mix from M&Ms, butterscotch flavoured pieces, carob-coated walnuts and raisins. That should pack a high-energy punch, I thought (it did but also turned out to be rather too sweet). Then,

33

on Warren Roger's recommendation, I visited two stalwarts of the Pacific Crest Club, Phil and Bing Le Fouvre, who kept the Wrightwood PCT Register and had a reputation for hospitality to long distance hikers. Sure enough they welcomed me in and let me take a bath (so much more soothing than a shower!) and wash my clothes (it would be chary to say this was in self-defence but I expect I did stink). When my fibre-pile jacket (for those curious fibre-pile was the precursor to fleece) came out of the drier I was amazed at how fluffy it was. I hadn't realised just how matted it had become. Leafing through the register I was interested to find two more British hikers who'd done the PCT.

That night I slept out in some woods at the edge of town. The night was warm and humid and for the first time my sleeping bag felt a little too hot. Traffic disturbed me early in the morning and when the first coffee shop opened for breakfast at 7 a.m. I was outside waiting. Full of a giant cooked breakfast I was then outside the Post Office when it opened. The contents of my parcel decanted into the pack I took the latter back to the Le Fouvre's to weigh it. 56lbs. That was with a week's food, 11/2 litres of white gas and two paperback books. I was pleased to see that there were four evening meals I hadn't tried yet in my supplies but disappointed that two of them required simmering for twenty-five minutes. Why ever had I bought those? It wasn't the time that bothered me but the fuel use. I just hoped they were tasty.

Wrightwood being a ski town with the Mountain High Resort just outside it I thought it might have an outdoor gear shop. It didn't. For the High Sierra I wanted crampons, gaiters and snowshoes. Maybe I would have to leave the trail to go out and buy them.

The climb back up to the PCT from Wrightwood took two hours. Heading uphill I took a better route and although steep the terrain didn't feel threatening. There followed several hours on a mix of trails and dirt roads past closed ski tows, the winter season being over, and closed campgrounds, the summer season not having started. The immediate environs weren't inspiring but looking back I could see Mount San Antonio while ahead was Mount Baden-Powell. I stopped for the day right at the start of the ascent of the latter in Vincent Gap and made camp under a spreading interior live oak tree by a snowmelt stream. Setting up camp had now become almost automatic. Lay out my groundsheet, inflate my sleeping mat, spread my sleeping bag out on it. The pack was propped up with my ice axe or propped against a tree. The stove was set up by the groundsheet. Once my water containers were full I could sit on the mat and relax, light the stove and make dinner. I loved

On Mount Baden-Powell with Dave and Scott

creating this little haven in the wilds each night. Camping is an important part of the backpacking experience for me and I liked to have time to enjoy staying in one place a short while and watch the wildlife and the landscape and the sky, especially when I could sleep under the stars and didn't need the tent. In fact one of the most delightful experiences of the whole walk was to lie under the trees listening to the quiet subtle sounds of the night and looking out to the distant lights of the universe. This spot was quite pleasant but sadly over-used with several blackened fire rings full of rusty cans and broken glass. The Angeles Crest Highway was not far away, making access easy in summer. Now the road was still closed for the winter so there was no traffic.

The previous day I'd seen three fresh sets of prints on the trail and suspected they might be from Scott, Dave and Larry. They tracks had vanished before I'd reached Vincent Gap though and I'd forgotten all about them until the next morning when I heard voices approaching as I ate breakfast. And there they were, having been camped just a few miles back. I must have walked right past. Having no ice axe or crampons Larry decided to walk the road round Mount Baden-Powell while Scott, Dave and I set off up the steep snowy mountain. The climb took us through pine and fir forest and then 2000 year old gnarled and wind-stunted limber pines. The snow was just soft enough to kick firm steps. This 9407 foot peak was the first real mountain of the walk and the view from the small summit was superb. Looking back I could see Mount San Antonio and Blue Ridge and, far in the distance now, San Gorgonio Peak and San Jacinto Peak. Ahead the mountain fell away to dusty foothills and the Mohave Desert. The sun was hot and the air sharp and crisp, making the summit a delightful place to linger. Unsurprisingly Mount Baden-Powell, named for the founder of the Boy Scouts back in the 1930s, is very popular with Scout groups when snow-free. There were no other people or even any tracks this early in the spring however.

Descent was on a neat little corniced ridge that undulated over a succession of lower summits. It was afternoon now and the sun was hot so the snow was soon soft and the going more arduous than on the ascent. Finally I realised it was easier to slide than trudge and had a 400 foot sitting glissade down to the highway at the bottom of the mountain. Here we camped at a closed picnic area, ignoring the sign that read No Overnight Camping. Soon after we'd set up camp we were surprised to be joined by two other PCT hikers, Gary and Tom, and their dog Hershey, who'd followed our tracks in the snow. It was nearly two weeks since we'd last met any other PCT hikers and we'd forgotten there were others on the trail. Writing in my journal by candlelight I noted 'Today possibly the best of the trip yet. A real mountain day'. We'd only walked ten miles but the distance didn't matter.

A mix of snowy hills, pine forests, sandy washes and chaparral occupied the next three days as we dipped in and out of mountains and desert. We met three more PCT hikers and only the second group of non-PCT hikers I'd seen. The walking was pleasant without being dramatic. My head was still on Mount Baden-Powell. A final descent, looking out over a cloud inversion to desert hills, took us to the old mining town of Acton where we found Larry and two PCT hikers who'd set off a month before me. Larry had a fresh salad and strawberries waiting for us, a delicious feast after all the days on dried food. Even better he'd met a local woman, Delree, who'd offered to give us a lift into Los Angeles the next day. I didn't particularly want to visit L.A. but this did solve my problem regarding gear for the High Sierra.

A strange day followed. An urban day of freeways, cars and buildings. We visited four outdoor stores in the San Fernando Valley. I spent $250 and came away with crampons, snowshoes, gaiters, insulated bootees, High Sierra topo maps, a quart water bottle to replace one that had cracked and, most pleasing of all, a copy of *The Sierra Club Naturalist's Guide to the Sierra Nevada.* Now I just had to carry it all across the Mohave Desert. Unusual though it was, the day off from hiking felt good. It was 17 days since my last one in Idyllwild.

Back in Acton other PCT hikers had arrived and soon there were eleven of us discussing the trail. The big Transverse Ranges lay behind us now. Ahead only the Mohave Desert separated us from the Sierra Nevada. Only the Mohave Desert, only excessive heat and lack of water, only a real desert. And then would come the snow. The Mohave Desert isn't the barren sandy desert of the imagination though. It's not the Sahara. Although it receives less than five inches of rain a year the Mohave is rich in plants and animals with over 250 species of the latter. I was looking forward to crossing it, though not to the heat.

Larry, Scott and Dave on the trail in the Sierra Pelona

Initially the walking was in more chaparral and dusty brush through the low Sierra Pelona Mountains. The air was hot and dry and we were thankful for the trickles of the last snowmelt water in the creeks, creeks that would be dry soon. There were many dirt roads and many dirt bikes roaring past with a stench of petrol. But there were also flowers, masses of

Top left: Flowers in the Mohave Desert
Right, bottom left and right:
Poppies in the Mohave Desert

flowers, especially tall yellow Western Wallflowers. On the second day out from Acton we saw our first rattlesnake, a big one, about four feet long, which rattled at Larry. It was the first of many and almost subconsciously I soon began avoiding long grass and the vicinity of bushes. Once when the tall grass was unavoidable we were walking on the narrow trail in single file when a loud rattle came from the grass at Larry's feet. Chaos ensued as Larry leapt backwards and collided heavily with Scott whilst Dave and I piled into the two of them. Then we saw the snake, a dark four foot long thickset coil that slowly straightened out and slid into the grass.

As we approached the flat expanse of the real desert the weather changed unexpectedly. It had been mostly hot and clear for over two weeks but overnight the skies greyed and we woke to a thick wet mist and moisture dripping off the trees and bushes. A day of drizzle, cold wind and low cloud followed. Again the flowers were the main joy of the walking, particularly the great swathes of bright orange poppies. The desert was in bloom, a short-lived event. Little settlements provided relief from the weather. At Lake Hughes we stocked up with the last food supplies for a while, and ate plenty too. At the Fairmont Inn Betty and Ralph Morgan cooked us a superb meal. We met few people but those we did were all friendly and curious about our walk. One local man gave us a half dozen fresh eggs each. That evening I broke four into my Mushroom Pilaf, keeping two for breakfast.

The route here and right across the Mohave Desert was a temporary one whilst negotiations went on with the large private Tejon Ranch for a permanent one. Today's route is very different from the one I hiked, the only place on the trail where this is so for any distance. Some books though still suggest that the route I took is preferable to the official one, which sounds very much a compromise. The crossing of the Mohave began on a dirt road signed 140th St.West which we followed for ten miles towards the distant Tehachapi Mountains, at first through alfalfa fields where sprinklers were running constantly and then out into the dry desert and the

In the Mohave Desert

Reading my way along a road in the Mohave Desert
Dave resting in the shade of a Joshua Tree in the Mohave Desert

first Joshua trees. I found these giant members of the yucca genus fascinating. Slightly sinister and slightly animate I kept expecting them to move. The biblical names comes from Mormon settlers who crossed the Mohave in the nineteenth century. On this long road section I read the natural history guide to the Sierra Nevada, which amused the others.

Across the Mohave there was a series of isolated homes whose residents had built up a network of overnight stops and water supply points for PCT hikers, an almost essential service. We were heading for a remote house belonging to an elderly lady called Mrs Davison who welcomed hikers. She made us coffee and let us sleep on her covered porch as rain still looked likely. The sky cleared though and a bright nearly full moon rose into the sky. In the distance we could see the lights of the desert towns of Lancaster and Palmdale. Wind chimes hung from the porch, their sound soothing and melodic in the warm desert wind.

Siesta by the Los Angeles Aqueduct in the Mohave Desert, Scott in the foreground getting water from the aqueduct via an inspection cap.

From Mrs Davison's the next thirty-five miles mostly followed the Los Angeles Aqueduct through an arm of the Mohave Desert known as Antelope Valley. The aqueduct was built in 1913 to bring water from Owens Valley below the High Sierra to rapidly growing and thirsty Los Angeles. Every mile there is an inspection cap and back in 1982 these could be opened (I believe most are now locked). There was just room to insert a water bottle and reach down and fill it with the cold rushing snowmelt water that was essential to Los Angeles and, at the time, to PCT hikers. Ten miles out from Mrs Davison's we stopped at one of these water sources and decided to sit out the heat of the day. We pitched our groundsheets as awnings to provide shade and cooled off by dowsing each other with the cold water. Under the awnings it was 27°C. In the sun it was much, much hotter.

41

Larry and Scott cooling off in the Mohave Desert

Rattlesnakes were common in the Mohave Desert. That first day we encountered four, including two big Mojave Greens. One of these lay in the middle of the dirt road and rattled aggressively at us, only moving when Scott lobbed stones towards it. After our siesta we saw two more that quickly slithered away as we walked into the night watching the sun set and the moon rise over the desert. We also saw large tortoises moving slowly over the stony ground. Finally after a 24-mile day we camped next to the Aqueduct. Despite the late night a bright moon and a strong gusty wind made sleep difficult and I was awake early to see a spectacular desert sunrise, the whole land glowing gold and red.

We were through the flat heart of the desert now and entering the foothills that would lead to the Sierra Nevada. This was still desert terrain though – the Mohave ranges in altitude from below sea level to over 8,000 feet – and still hot and dry. Tiny settlements provided liquid and breaks from the heat – Cinco, which started out as a work camp for workers on the Aqueduct, where we had a meal at Spragues Restaurant, the only building, then Cantil, founded as a station on the Nevada and California Railroad, which had a good little store and a post office. At the last place we sat out the heat of the day again, resting from noon until late afternoon and drinking fruit juice and eating enchiladas and ice cream. Another PCT hiker wandered in. Wayne Fuiten was ex-military and highly organised, clicking off every step on a counter, resting for five minutes every hour and averaging nineteen miles a day. He'd left Campo nine days after me and had taken no rest days. So far I'd had three. We were to see Wayne frequently over the next three days and I was to meet him again in northern Oregon but we never hiked together as my random stops and widely varying daily mileages couldn't have fitted with his organised progress.

Continuing along the aqueduct after our siesta we eventually camped beside it in Jawbone Canyon. I just loved these Western names! I pitched the tent to keep the wind off but slept on top of my sleeping bag because of the heat. I was looking forward to cooler nights. They would come as the trail was climbing now, up through pleasant high desert mountains past Butterbredt Spring, a nice spot with cottonwood trees and a small pool, and along Butterbredt Canyon to Butterbredt Well, where there was a windmill to pump the water. The water in the well was green and polluted by cattle but we managed to extract clean water from the inlet pipe. The repeated occurrence of the name Butterbredt made me wonder just where it came from. Research after the walk revealed a German immigrant called Frederick Butterbredt who prospected in the area in the late 1860s and whose descendants lived in the area for many years.*

The day ended under more cottonwoods beside Kelso Creek (cottonwoods are a type of poplar that grows by water – I was to learn on other desert walks that the sight of cottonwoods in the distance meant there would probably be water there). People from a nearby house, the Plants, gave us fresh water. The scenery was pleasant, the walking not difficult and there were still masses of flowers. Even so I would be glad to leave the desert. The heat was overwhelming and the sandy landscape changed very slowly at walking pace. Never having been to a desert before I'd been excited at the thought of hiking through one and was glad I'd experienced it. Now though I was excited at the thought of leaving it. I also felt elated because at Kelso Creek I passed the 500-mile mark. I could let myself be excited too as only nineteen miles remained to the town of Weldon, which since Campo had meant the end of the beginning, the end of the initiation and the start of the Range of Light, the magical Sierra Nevada. The knowledge

43

Clockwise:
Camp in the Mohave Desert
Bird Spring Pass on the southern edge of the Sierra Nevada
The desert in bloom

that these mountains were still snowbound and as far as I knew no-one had yet hiked the PCT through them this year only added spice to my anticipation. These were the mountains that had sparked the whole adventure and now I was almost there.

We were three thousand feet higher than Jawbone Canyon and thankfully that meant a cooler night. I fell asleep watching bats flying round the cottonwoods. The last desert day saw a change in the weather, which felt like a welcome to the mountains, and it was very windy and quite cold. The walk to Weldon was along a road, hard on the feet but fast, and with the weather keeping us moving we were soon there. Weldon was a dusty little town strung out along the highway. We established a base at the KOA Campground, which was to be home for three nights as we spent two days in Weldon. Apart from one small store at Kennedy Meadows this was the last place I'd see for twenty-six days so it was here that preparations for the snow and the

Chronology

mountains were made. I collected my supply parcel from the post office and was delighted to find five tubes of glacier cream, which I'd need in the sun and the snow at high altitude, and excited by Warren's maps and the next sections of the trail guide. Scott and Dave collected skis, which they'd stashed here when they drove over from home. Larry's snow gear arrived, sent from his home, so he would be able to come through the Sierra. Wayne however, who turned up soon after us, was going to hitch-hike round the Sierra, intending to return and hike this section after the snow had melted. I guessed his strict schedule wouldn't work in high snowy terrain. Another PCT hiker, Ken, who I'd first met in Idyllwild, had changed his mind about going through the snow and was going to walk roads round the Sierra. We'd met no-one else who was planning on hiking through the snow.

The weather in Weldon was chilly and damp, with drizzle and the occasional rumble of thunder. What would it be like up in the mountains? Soon we would know.

*More information can be found on the Desert Explorer website – http://www.dustyway.com/2007/09/pioneer-frederick-butterbredt.html

THROUGH SNOW & HIGH WATER:
THE HIGH SIERRA

WELDON TO ECHO LAKE
May 12 to June 24
429 miles

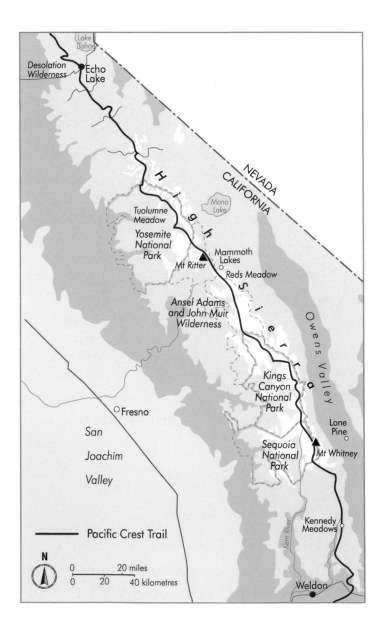

Lake Tahoe

Desolation Wilderness

Echo Lake

NEVADA

CALIFORNIA

High

Mono Lake

Tuolumne Meadow

Yosemite National Park

Mammoth Lakes

Mt Ritter

Reds Meadow

Ansel Adams and John Muir Wilderness

S i e r r a

Kings Canyon National Park

Owens Valley

Lone Pine

Fresno

San Joachim Valley

Sequoia National Park

Mt Whitney

Kern River

Kennedy Meadows

—— Pacific Crest Trail

N

| 0 | | 20 miles |
| 0 | 20 | 40 kilometres |

Weldon

The Sierra Nevada was first named by Spanish sailors who saw the distant range of jagged snow-capped mountains from their ships. A sierra is a serrated mountain range, nevada means snowy. The range stretches for some four hundred miles, of which two hundred towards the southern end of the range constitute the High Sierra. Essentially the High Sierra is a huge tilted block of granite with the steep scarp slope on the east side, dropping some 9,000 feet to Owens Valley. On the gentler western side the mountains slowly dwindle away to forested foothills. The High Sierra contains Mount Whitney, at 14,505 feet the highest summit in the 48 contiguous States, which I was hoping to climb, and Lake Tahoe, the largest alpine lake in North America. There are also three national parks, including world-famous Yosemite, twenty wilderness areas and two national monuments. This is the land of Scottish-American naturalist and conservationist John Muir who explored it from the 1860s and fought for its preservation. It was Muir who gave it the name Range of Light. I'd barely heard of Muir when I hiked the PCT as he was little known in Britain then. However with the John Muir Wilderness and the John Muir Trail in the High Sierra I soon realised he was a significant figure. The PCT follows much of the 210 mile John Muir Trail.

For the next 290 miles and 34 days I would not cross a road and would only resupply twice on the edge of the mountains. The longest single section between supply points was 200 miles and took 22 days. I'd never spent anything like that long in wild country without a break before and I was looking forward to it with excitement. This was the wilderness heart of the PCT. This was the landscape that had inspired my walk. This was the land I had come to experience.

Although geologically the Sierra Nevada starts well south of Weldon and we'd been walking through it for several days there was no sign of this in the desert landscape. From Weldon the trail started to climb and the landscape slowly changed to forest so I really felt I was finally leaving the chaparral and desert country behind. The High Sierra was still some fifty miles away but I was returning to the mountains and glad to be doing so. My first journal entry for the day I left Weldon reads 'back in the hills!' Soon after setting off we climbed into cool Jeffery pine forest. By the end of the day we'd climbed 4,500 feet onto the Kern Plateau.

Black bears are common in the Sierra Nevada and in popular areas may raid campsites for food. Never having been in bear country before I felt nervous about encountering one of these animals. On this first day in the range it wasn't a bear that caused problems though but a

47

With Larry and Dave in the High Sierra

domestic bull. We were on a dirt road with steep slopes either side when we rounded a bend to see a large bull standing in the middle of the track. On seeing us he shook his head, snorted and began pawing the ground. With amazing speed given our big packs Scott, Dave and I dropped down a slope into dense undergrowth. Larry edged round the bull, which thankfully didn't charge. This was brave certainly but also probably unwise. The three of us bushwhacked through the undergrowth until we were well past the beast.

The only other danger came from creatures the opposite in size to the bull. On accidentally turning over a small rock I found two pale gold scorpions, the only ones I saw on the trail. There was other wildlife too. Red-winged blackbirds darted through the trees, looking similar to the blackbirds of home apart from the distinctive red markings, while overhead a red-tailed hawk soared, again reminding me of home as it is very similar to the common buzzard.

We camped that night in the woods at 6600 feet, the highest for two weeks. It would be nearly fifty days before I camped below 6000 feet again. The crisp cool air was welcome and I felt I could return to sleeping properly at night. By dawn the temperature was only just above freezing.

So far on the walk most days had gone roughly according to plan. The next one didn't. After only a mile or so we lost the trail when it faded out in a big meadow. Unable to locate it anywhere we ended up following some orange plastic flagging on a very circuitous route that did eventually lead back to the trail. After four hours steady walking we'd progressed just five miles along the PCT. Then I discovered I'd lost my compass, which I'd been using to ensure we at least walked in the right direction when not on the trail, and along with it my safety whistle, which was on the same length of cord. If that wasn't enough I then broke a camera. I'd brought a clamp with a camera attachment that I could fasten to posts and branches to take self-portrait and low light pictures. So far it had worked fine but using it that day the screw went right through the base of the camera. The shutter then jammed open and the light meter wouldn't turn off. I was relieved I'd brought two camera bodies and vowed not to use the clamp again. The day did end with a fine campsite amongst superb Jeffrey pines, white firs and lodgepole pines. There was no snow yet but the meadows were mostly flooded and the ground sodden from recent snowmelt.

The first snow came the next day on 9350 foot Siretta Pass where there were also some magnificent gnarled limber pines, which I hadn't seen since Mount Baden-Powell. Scott skied for the first time, which I found fascinating. I didn't know you could use skis for backpacking. All I knew about skiing was that it was something done at noisy, crowded resorts with much ironmongery, which didn't interest me at all. I hadn't come across ski touring or cross-country skiing. Watching Scott and Dave over the next weeks I realised it was an ideal way to travel on

Journal Entry

snow. Snowshoes, as used by Larry and me, were okay but much slower. I wanted to glide rather than plod. The next winter I would take a course in the Scottish Highlands, after which skiing would be a regular activity when there was snow.

We were now on the Kern Plateau and in the Domeland Wilderness. The reason for the latter name was obvious as we walked below a wall of granite domes, spires and cliffs rising out of the forest. Once out of the snow the ground was sodden again and we had the first of what would be many creek fords in the Sierra Nevada. Little Trout Creek was thigh-deep and very cold but the water was slow and the bed firm. The next day started abruptly after a frosty night with an equally deep ford of equally slow Fish Creek beyond which we soon reached the big South Fork of the Kern River. We didn't have to try and ford this though but instead followed it to the roadhead and bridge at Kennedy Meadows where there was a Forest Service campground and a store that held parcels for PCT hikers. Here I had a box containing dinners for 18 days. It weighed nearly 17lbs. I added a bit more as I suspected it might take longer than 18 days to reach the next supply point given the snow and then doubled the weight with breakfast and lunch foods. Although this resulted in a pack I could hardly lift I was to be glad I had so much food as the next section was to take 22 days. I was also delighted to receive my first letter from home, posted 27 days earlier. I'd been away from home for 46 days without any contact until now, which is hard to believe in this age of text messages and email. I could have phoned of course but the cost was prohibitive and friends and family knew I would only do so in an emergency. It would be three weeks before I could send a reply as there was no postal service from

The heaviest load – with 23 days supplies in the Southern Sierra Nevada

Fording the Kern River, Southern Sierra Nevada
Hanging food out of reach of bears, High Sierra

Kennedy Meadows. My main form of communication was postcards, some of which I sent from each post office.

Having reached Kennedy Meadows quite early in the day we didn't stay but walked a few miles alongside the South Fork of the Kern River and camped in the forest. In the store we'd been told that a black bear had hassled a hiker in this area recently so we hung our food for the first time, a procedure known as bear bagging. This proved quite difficult with food sacks weighing some 30lbs. It was essential in some areas though, especially further ahead in the High Sierra. Black bears are common in the Sierra Nevada and in popular areas have learnt that hikers' food is quite tasty. Protecting food also protects the bears as ones that become used to human foodstuffs can lose their fear of people and become a danger so they have to be caught and relocated or even shot. Indeed, it's to protect bears that there are now regulations regarding food storage.

51

Today many areas of the High Sierra require hikers to use large plastic food containers that bears cannot break into. However these bear-resistant containers, sometimes known as bear barrels, didn't exist back in 1982 and hanging food high in trees was the only way to keep it safe from bears. Sierra bears are clever though and just throwing a line over a branch, hauling up a food bag and tying the other end of the line round the tree trunk is ineffective as the bears have learnt that if they find a line and break it a food bag will appear. This isn't true in other areas and on later trips I used this method in the Canadian Rockies, the Yukon Territory and other places and never lost my food.

In the High Sierra a more complex method, known as counterbalancing, was required. Setting this up was tedious and could be time-consuming. It involved finding a branch at least fifteen feet above the ground, throwing a cord over it tied to the end of a stone, hauling a food bag up to the branch, tying another bag of equal weight to the other end of the cord and then hurling that bag into the air in the hope that the two bags would end up side by side at least ten feet above the ground and five feet away from the trunk of the tree (bears can climb). There was much that could go wrong with this. Cords could get tangled up round branches and branches could break. Stones would fly off into the distance. Sometimes it could take time to find a suitable branch. Popular campsites could be identified not just by bare ground and fire rings but also by lengths of cord hanging out of reach from branches. I quickly learnt that it was best to set up the system as soon as I made camp and before I relaxed too much so that after eating all I had to do was haul up my food bags. I hated doing it but losing my precious food to a bear did not appeal. Mornings were worst as I had to leave my warm sleeping bag and rescue my food from its tree – usually by jumping up and down with my ice axe until I could snag one of the bags – before I could have breakfast. This disrupted my preferred morning camp ritual which involved lighting the stove and making coffee and drinking this with breakfast – usually granola – before leaving the sleeping bag. However in case I was tempted to not bother hanging my food the regular fresh bear tracks and droppings encountered every few days were a good reminder.

For the next three days we slowly climbed through the southern Sierra Nevada, gradually gaining height and encountering more and more snow. From the South Fork of the Kern River the trail led through open forest with some magnificent Incense Cedar trees to the vast Monache Meadows above which rose impressive triangular rocky 12,123 foot Olancha Peak, the first of the big Sierra

Camp by the South Fork of the Kern River in the Southern Sierra Nevada
Dave and Scott carrying skis across Monache Meadows in the Southern Sierra Nevada

peaks. There was little snow on the south and west slopes of this mountain but we knew that deeper into the Sierra Nevada we would find plenty. Although we'd been on snow-free trails and there hadn't been much ascent it had taken seven hours to walk eleven miles and that was enough with our very heavy packs so we stopped and made camp. I really felt the weight on my hips and shoulders and my ankles were aching. 'Still, it's getting lighter every day' I wrote in my journal. I was to think that many times in coming days. That evening I lay and watched a beautiful pastel shaded delicate slow sunset, all pinks and pale orange. The natural world was already a reward for the effort of carrying the pack. Here with the forest and meadows all around and Olancha Peak rising high above I really felt I was in the Sierra Nevada for the first time. The thought of the many weeks of this to come sent a shiver of excitement through me.

Dawn came with a heavy frost. Everything was white. A drifting mist wreathed river and rocks and meadow. It was a beautiful start to the day. A climb led up to a saddle on the side of Olancha Peak. At 10,500 feet it was the first time I'd been above 10,000 feet on this walk. Now much of the next three weeks would be above that altitude. On the saddle were many weather-beaten foxtail pines, a rare tree that is only found high in the mountains in California. The name comes from its thick bundles of long needles, which resemble a fox's tail. Unsurprisingly at this height

53

On the Sierra Crest with Owens Valley far below

there was also snow though it was patchy and we could still follow the trail. Descending from the saddle the snow became deeper with a breakable crust. This is awful stuff to walk on, or rather through, as each step collapses when you put weight on it. With our heavy packs the going was hard work and slow. Again we only made eleven miles before camping but this time it had taken nine hours. We were not going to get through the Sierra Nevada quickly. Another first came with the camp. It was the highest of the walk so far at 9,000 feet.

Again we climbed on mostly snow free slopes but descended in deep snow on the north side. The ascent led to a ridge that gave our dramatic first view 9,000 feet down to Owens Valley and the pink alkaline flats of Owens Lake. This lake is now mostly dry because its water was diverted through the Los Angeles Aqueduct along which we'd walked across the desert. In the snow I

View down to Owens Valley from the crest of the High Sierra
On snowshoes in the High Sierra forests

finally wore for the first time the snowshoes that I'd been carrying for fifteen days. I'd never used snowshoes before and had no idea how to do so. I quickly discovered that they were fine on flat terrain as long as I remembered to walk with a wide-legged cowboy waddle but that they slipped rather easily on slopes. That was until I realised I should kick my toes into the snow. The boot attachments were hinged and had crude points, called 'sno-claws' under them for grip on ice, so I could push these into the snow while the actual snowshoe lay flat on the surface. The snowshoes were essential. Without them I'd have spent exhausting hours postholing through deep snow and my progress would have been much slower. On gentle slopes and uneven terrain balancing on the snowshoes was sometimes difficult though as I didn't have any poles for support. Trekking poles didn't exist back then and, not being a skier, it never occurred to me that ski poles would have been very useful. On steep slopes I could use my ice axe but this was too short elsewhere. Larry didn't use poles either, nor had Scott or Dave in the Southern California mountains. If they had I'd probably have bought some. On their skis Scott and Dave soon left Larry and me far behind.

Late in the day we climbed towards another saddle where we planned on camping. The snow was soft now after many hours in the hot sun and even with the snowshoes and skis we sank in it. Learning from this we realised we should set off at dawn and stop mid-afternoon and that ideally climbs, which were south-facing, should be done early in the day. The PCT in the Sierra Nevada followed a fairly regular pattern of ascents to high passes followed by descent back into the forest and then another ascent. A daily routine was soon established, unlike further south where constant changes from chaparral to desert to forest to mountains had meant very different days with no consistent pattern to them. In the Sierra Nevada we rose before dawn to cook and eat breakfast in the usually freezing air while waiting for the first warming rays of the sun. Many nights we camped on snow and most nights the temperature dropped below zero though never lower than -10ºC. This meant the snow early in the day would be rock hard – 'Sierra cement' as it's known – and we often needed crampons for security. Later in the day we'd try and get as close to the next pass as possible before the snow became too soft and we gave up and camped.

Progress through the High Sierra was arduous and we averaged only ten miles a day. The landscape though was glorious and worth all the pain and effort. Range after range of golden granite peaks of every shape and form soared above the snowfields and the deep wooded canyons down which crashed wild creeks from the still-frozen alpine lakes, the water surging out from under the ice. For a lover of wilderness and natural beauty this was a perfect world. Ten miles a day would remain the average for the next 200 miles, all the way to our next supply point, Mammoth Lakes. The magical, wonderful, unbelievable wild world would last all that way too. We were above 10,000 feet virtually the whole way and often camped above 11,000 feet. Timberline in the High Sierra is around 10,500 feet so sometimes we dipped down into the alpine forest of foxtail, whitebark and lodgepole pines but most of the time we were above the trees in a monochrome world of black and grey rocks and white snow with the only colours coming from the blue of the sky and the changing sun, which went from dark red to orange to gold to yellow to white and back again. Although the landscape was complex our days followed a repeating pattern. Forest, snow-filled canyon, mountain pass again and again and again, a sequence of which I never tired.

As we progressed northwards I came to particularly love timberline, that area where the trees thinned out and grew smaller and the forest gradually merged with the open mountainside. Timberline was not static, it rose and fell with the shape of the land, the aspect of the slope (higher on the south and west facing slopes, lower on those to the north and east) and the underlying terrain. The types of trees and their size varied too. In some places the forest ended fairly abruptly in a ragged line of tall trees, in others small trees continued to grow high above the forest proper. The variety was a delight on the eye and kept the landscape always interesting. It was a stark contrast to the forests of home, which were mostly plantations in rigid blocks. Even the few natural forests left in the hills were generally curtailed below the natural timberline due to overgrazing by deer and sheep. Only in a handful of places in the Scottish hills was there a real timberline and nowhere could it be seen extending mile after mile after mile. However although I was familiar with the woods in the hills of Britain it was only after seeing these Sierra Nevada forests and the forests that lay ahead on the PCT that I realised just how damaged or unnatural they

Crossing early morning 'Sierra cement'

mostly were and how much regeneration and restoration was needed to bring them back to a wild and natural state. Ever since the PCT I have supported those organisations working to do this such as Trees for Life, the Woodland Trust and the Royal Society for the Protection of Birds. The Sierra mountains were magnificent but life lay in the beauty of the forests.

All that was lacking were animals and birds but that was due to the time of year. Wildlife sightings were uncommon because most creatures would be down in the forest below the snowline where there was food and warmth. We did see many yellow-bellied marmots basking on rocks. These large bulky rodents were a common sight around rock fields and scree slopes and would stand on their hind legs and whistle loudly on seeing us before diving for cover in holes between the boulders.

Overleaf: Ski and snowshoe tracks

Out of the snow – crossing granite slabs in the High Sierra

We approached the High Sierra over the mostly snow free Mulkey Pass and Trail Pass. Mount Langley, the southernmost of the twelve peaks over 14,000 feet in the Sierra Nevada, came into view. From the climb to Cottonwood Pass, regarded as the start of the High Sierra, the views were stupendous. Beyond the pass we camped at Chicken Spring Lake at 11,242 feet, the highest camp I'd ever had. So far the altitude hadn't affected me and I was hoping this would continue as there were higher passes to come. The way the PCT unfolds helps with acclimatising to altitude as the height only gradually increases and the first sections above 10,000 feet are only short. By the time I reached the High Sierra I had been high enough often enough that my body was starting to acclimatise. In fact the altitude didn't affect me noticeably at all.

This camp was also the finest of the trip so far. A curving ridge with a cornice, cliffs and scree hung above the lake, which was frozen solid. I felt in the heart of the mountains, remote from the world below with snowy peaks all around.

Camp at Chicken Spring Lake, High Sierra

Now we were mostly in the snow the trail was invisible, with only tree blazes and other signs indicating its presence. At first we still tried to follow it but often it traversed steep slopes that were difficult in the snow, especially when it was icy. On the day out from Chicken Spring Lake we looked down to the flat plain called Siberian Outpost and decided to cross that rather than stick with the trail which ran through steep woods. After this, whilst we stayed close to the line of the trail, we took what looked like the easiest route in the snow, which often meant crossing meadows and valley bottoms – sometimes across the middle of frozen lakes – rather than traversing slopes. During the day we entered the southernmost of the High Sierra's national parks, Sequoia, which was created in part to protect the magnificent Giant Sequoia trees that grow on the western edge of the High Sierra. These are far from the PCT and I didn't have time to make a diversion to see them. Many years later I came back and did a 500 mile circular walk from Yosemite Valley to see the Giant Sequoias and other places I'd missed on the PCT including

61

Snowshoeing across Siberian Outpost, High Sierra

King's Canyon and Yosemite Valley itself. One of the few restrictions on a long walk is the need to stick to the route most of the time. I knew I had to reach Canada before the first snows of the next winter made the going dangerous and maybe impassable (and also before my six-month Visa ran out). Giant Forest where the big Sequoias grow was just too far away to visit.

Down in the forest the creeks were mostly open, making for some cold though not usually hazardous fords, though there was occasionally a snowbridge still strong enough to bear our weight. When I was wearing them I sometimes waded across in my snowshoes – one of the few advantages they had over skis. They were also easier to carry in the trees as they didn't stick out high above my head but otherwise the skis were clearly the better way to travel. If our boots were still dry – mine were usually soaked by the end of the day and still damp in the morning – we wore running shoes for creek crossings. This nearly resulted in a disaster at Rock Creek below Siberian Outpost when Dave dropped one of his ski boots into the water and it was rapidly washed away. We searched along the banks and eventually I spotted it trapped against a log jam and managed to retrieve it after a slimy and slippery crawl out on a thin branch. We were many days from a road and hiking in running shoes would not have been easy or pleasant in the snow. After that incident I made sure I tied my boots to the pack rather than carried them in my hand. That night we camped by the creek at 9400 feet, which already felt quite low.

We were now only seven miles from Crabtree Meadows, a starting point for the ascent of Mount Whitney. We all wanted to climb this mountain and had agreed to take a day off from the trail for this. It was one diversion I wasn't going to miss. Although not on the Pacific Crest Trail Whitney is the southern terminus of the John Muir Trail. As with all highest mountains in a region or country (even Mount Everest these days) it is popular and in the summer there is a permit system and numbers are strictly regulated – a few weeks after our ascent we heard that the mountain was already fully booked for the coming summer. We would avoid all of this. When we'd asked a ranger about the need for permits for the national parks in the High Sierra and about camping restrictions he'd just told us the parks were closed and that we could go if we wanted but there were no rangers and no support. We'd be on our own, which was fine with us.

At Crabtree Meadows, which we reached at lunchtime, we found a good site on snow free ground under some lodgepole pines with a view across the meadows to the soaring spires of Mount Young, Mount Hitchcock and the serrated Mount Whitney Pinnacles. A white snowshoe hare darted across the open meadows as we watched the mountains. 'A superb site, perhaps the best yet', I wrote in my journal. There were to be many more contenders for this in the High Sierra.

Mount Whitney would be a long and steep climb. I was familiar with using ice axe and crampons and had done a little snow and ice mountaineering as had Scott and Dave. Larry hadn't however so as he was determined to come on the climb I spent a few hours at Crabtree Meadows teaching him the rudiments of ice axe use. This was hardly an adequate preparation for an ascent of a remote high wilderness mountain but it was all that was possible. Scott and Dave skied round the meadows, free to speed along gracefully without their heavy packs. Watching them convinced me I had to learn how to ski.

Late in the afternoon there was a sudden build-up of dark massive cumulo-nimbus clouds over the main Sierra crest. Soon the threatened thunderstorm began though no rain fell on our camp. It raged for the next three hours, a dramatic sight, before fading away as the sun set, leaving the last clouds to turn pink. This storm convinced us we needed a very early start for Mount Whitney as the thought of being up high in such weather was terrifying so we were awake at the ghastly hour of 4.30 a.m. and off by six on the 18-mile round trip. More significant than the distance was the ascent though, which was over 4,000 feet.

A walk up a narrow canyon under glaciated rock walls led to a traverse of steep icy slopes where crampons were needed. Next came a series of switchbacks that were only partially snow-covered

On the ascent of Mount Whitney

and which led to the main ridge at Trail Crest. We were now in the heart of alpine wildness far above the forest. All around were superb glaciated cirques laced with snow gullies and topped by rock ridges and pinnacles. Ignoring the partially hidden trail we made a direct ascent on scree to Trail Crest. Back on the trail we now followed the crest towards the summit, winding between sharp pinnacles above the granite-lined cirques and with, far below, the tiny circles of frozen lakes and the dark spread of the forest. Between the pinnacles there were dizzying views straight down to Owens Valley. The narrow path was often snow covered and precarious, especially where it was steeply banked up with snow round the bulging sides of the buttresses. Here we could teeter round on our crampons, facing inwards and clinging perilously to the rock. In a few places I'd have felt much safer with a rope and a belay. This felt like real mountaineering.

Eventually the crest widened out to a vast snowfield that lead easily to the summit. The view was huge. The High Sierra was spread out around us with the sharp rock ridges and peaks of endless snow-spattered mountains rising above vast snow-filled basins. To the east the mountain fell away precipitately to the shimmering pale desert. Away to the west a big thunderstorm was raging.

We spent an hour on the summit taking in the view and recovering from the climb. The altitude had affected me less than I thought it might and I only felt slightly breathless but even so a rest was welcome. Also, this was the highest mountain I'd ever climbed. I didn't want to dash away, especially with such a stupendous view. This was wilderness! At this time of year anyway as there were signs of the summer – a toilet shed and a concrete ice-filled shelter – which I did my best to ignore. A brass USGS benchmark disk marked the height as 14, 494 feet (current measurements make it 14,505 feet). There's nothing higher in the USA outside Alaska.

On approaching the mountain we'd noticed several snow-filled gullies running down from the west face of the mountain. To speed up the descent and avoid the scary traverse below the pinnacles we decided to descend one of these. First we dropped down the summit snowfield and then a long slope of bare talus that led to the top of the narrow, twisting gullies. From above we couldn't see all the way down any of them. Finally we selected one that looked reasonably safe for a sitting glissade – sliding down the snow on our backsides with the ice axe ready to use as a brake. We went one at a time to avoid crashing into each other. Dave first, soon followed by Scott, both of them reappearing on the wide snow slope at the bottom. Then Larry set off. I watched as he picked up speed rather too rapidly and then vanished round the first kink in the gully in a cloud of flying snow and stones. There was a loud yell then silence. There was no sign of Larry where the others had appeared. I waited, shocked. Thoughts raced through my mind. Was Larry injured? Was he even still alive? Finally, after what seemed an age though was probably only a minute or so, I heard a faint cry – 'I've lost my ice axe!' Unable to see where Larry was and not wanting to collide with him I scrambled carefully down the loose rock beside the gully. Where he'd lost control there were stones sticking out of the snow. Not far to the side I found his ice axe wedged between two rocks. Below Larry lay spread-eagled on his back in the middle of the slope. I called out to him, asking if he could move to the side of the gully so I wouldn't crash into him if I glissaded down. He started to move but immediately slipped and lay still again. Rather than risk a collision I climbed down, kicking steps in the hard snow and using the two ice axes as daggers

View down a gully on Mount Whitney
Glissading down the gully on Mount Whitney

to support myself. I could have done with crampons but they were strapped on the back of Larry's pack – we'd only taken one pack between us as we hadn't much to carry. In fact the two pairs of crampons on the pack were probably what had stopped Larry's slide.

When I reached Larry I found him shaken but without injury other than a grazed hand. He didn't want to glissade anymore though so we slowly descended kicking steps and using the ice axes for security until the angle eased off and he felt able to slide the last few hundred feet. Finally and with great relief we reached Scott and Dave who had been watching from below and wondering what was going on. We'd been very lucky. A serious accident days away from any help could have had unthinkable consequences. We plodded back to camp, arriving tired but pleased after a thirteen hour day.

Back in camp we found a note from two PCT hikers, Phil and Andy, who'd passed by on skis. Perhaps, we thought, we might have tracks to follow until the sun obliterated them, at least for a few days. Our morning tracks had already softened though and would soon be gone. Even on the top of Mount Whitney the snow was thawing. We weren't too surprised when Phil and Andy's tracks were barely visible the next day. After the long arduous day on Mount Whitney we were

Mount Whitney from the Bighorn Plateau, High Sierra

happy to have a somewhat easier day though we were still in snow virtually the whole time. We were also mostly in dense trees and for once snowshoes were more manoeuvrable than skis and for the first and only time Larry and I had to wait an hour for Scott and Dave to catch up on a wooded saddle. The day was most memorable for the view from the vast open space of the Bighorn Plateau, which was ringed by wonderfully rugged and ragged rock peaks. Looking back we could see Mount Whitney soaring steeply into the sky. It was hard to believe we had stood on top just the day before. To the west lay another impressive wall of granite peaks, the Great Western Divide, which runs parallel to the main Sierra crest. Ahead the Kings-Kern Divide, so-called because it is the watershed between the Kings and Kern rivers, linked the two. Tomorrow we would cross this great rock ridge via the highest pass on the PCT, 13,180 foot Forester Pass. This is the first in a series of high passes crossed by the PCT in quick succession. Remembering the thunderstorm we planned to be over each of them in the mornings, which meant more really early starts.

View from the tent at the camp by Tyndall Creek, the day before crossing Forester Pass

The day on Forester Pass was helped by camping at almost 11,000 feet the night before. This left half the amount of ascent we'd had on the climb of Mount Whitney. Against that we were carrying full packs. Awake before dawn at 5 a.m. the day began with Scott and Dave setting their stove ablaze. We were all using white gas stoves that required priming by lighting liquid fuel to get them going. Still half-asleep Scott and Dave had failed to close the fuel tank on their stove so when they lit the priming fuel the flame quickly spread to the tank and the whole stove went up in a ball of fire. All they could do was sit and watch a tankful of fuel burn away. The stove wasn't damaged though and no-one was hurt. It woke us all up too! This event was soon forgotten as the day unfolded, a day I was to describe as 'another epic day' in my journal.

The approach to Forester Pass was through barren snowy and rocky ground past frozen lakes. Ahead the Kings-Kern Divide was a solid rock wall that looked impassable. In fact there is a

The south side of Forester Pass
Crossing the gully on Forester Pass

trail that was blasted into the rock in 1930. Initially steep crampon work led up frozen snow to the start of the switchbacks up the rock face. These were snow free and made for easy walking until the trail crossed a snow-filled gully not far from the top of the pass. Half the gully was in sunlight, half in shadow. The snow in the sun was fairly soft, that in the shadow rock hard. Dave and Scott crossed the gully and continued up the switchbacks, here quite snowy, to the top. I'd noticed that when they crossed the sunny section Dave and Scott had set off little snow slides, which made me concerned about the possibility of an avalanche. That still doesn't explain my stupidity however. For some reason when I reached the edge of the sunny section I decided to try and climb straight up the gully on the front points of my crampons. It was only about forty feet but trying to climb that distance up very steep hard snow at 13,000 feet with one ice axe, bendy boots and a pack weighing around 70lbs is not sensible. I managed though until a final

69

Charlotte Dome in the High Sierra near Bubbs Creek

corniced vertical section of soft snow stopped me. I could make no progress up this, sliding back as my footholds collapsed. I was stuck. Rescue came from above. Dave lowered down his ice axe on the 5mm line Scott was carrying, mostly for river crossings. I tied the cord round my waist and was belayed from above. With Dave and Scott heaving on the rope and by pulling up on the two ice axes thrust into the snow above me I managed to plough my way up to the cornice. A helping hand enabled me to squirm inelegantly onto the pass where I lay panting and very relieved. Larry, waiting patiently below, wisely decided to follow Scott and Dave and take the sensible route.

Forester Pass is a narrow notch on a rocky crest that is the border between Sequoia and Kings Canyon National Parks. We were now in the heartland of the High Sierra. Rock and snow peaks rolled away before and behind us. Thankfully the descent was easy, just a tramp down snowfields on snowshoes to roaring Bubbs Creek with excellent views of a series of rock spires called the Kearsage Pinnacles. We camped in the woods beside the creek on the edge of Vidette Meadows with another superb view, this time of East Vidette, a massive triangular rock peak that reminded me of Buachaille Etive Mor, one of the most distinctive and impressive mountains in the Scottish Highlands.

The next few days would give me an opportunity to experience the High Sierra in solitude. Scott and Dave had cached supplies in Onion Valley on the east side of the mountains and were planning on going out to collect them the next day and spend a night down below. As there was a store there Larry was going with them. I didn't want to leave the mountains and break their spell so I agreed to look after the tents and other gear so they could travel light. I handed Larry a shopping list, mostly of day snacks as, despite the huge load I'd carried from Kennedy Meadows, I'd run out. From Vidette Meadows we clambered over avalanche debris below the Kearsage Pinnacles and followed a stream to mostly frozen Bullfrog Lake where we found Phil and Andy just packing up. They too were going down to Onion Valley. By mid-morning I was alone.

Bullfrog Lake was in a beautiful situation at timberline with a few gnarled whitebark and lodgepole pines half-buried in the snow dotted around and mountains rising in every direction. Clark's nutcrackers, rosy finches and mountain chickadees flitted through the trees. The snow was deep but thawing fast. Whilst walking we'd not really been aware of just how quickly it was going but now it became very apparent. Larry had pitched his tent to store all their gear so I had two tents to look after. And they did need looking after as every few hours they began to sag as the snow round them melted and the pegs pulled out. Soon they were sitting on platforms several inches thick as the snow under them didn't melt. I lay outside on my insulating mat reading and writing my journal some of the time but mostly just watching the mountains and the trees and the sky and the snow. I relished this time alone and without any pressure to move on. I could just relax and be here in the wilderness.

This stationary sojourn in the mountains gave a different perspective to the Sierra Nevada and to the journey. I noticed details missed when on the move – how the shadows changed as the sun moved across the sky, how at different times the light picked out tree bark, rock walls, the curves in the snow. I was static. The world was not. That night I could hear coyotes howling not far away. I woke to a heavy frost coating the inside and outside of the tent. Unable to go far

Camp by Bullfrog Lake with cloud over Kearsage Pass

because of the tents I wandered round the lake watching the open water increase in size as the snow and ice thawed, crossing creeks on diminishing snow bridges and staring at the peaks. In the afternoon clouds built-up and shrouded the peaks. A cool breeze sprang up. Soon a steady drizzle was falling, the first rain for forty-four days. I had expected the others back late in the day but they didn't appear. When the rain stopped I wandered towards Kearsage Pass, which they'd crossed, to see if they were coming. A snow bridge over a creek they'd crossed had gone, leaving rushing water ten feet wide. Their boot prints had vanished. As the skies cleared at dusk a thin crescent moon appeared and the last clouds hanging over Kearsage Pass turned pink. There was no sign of the others.

During my two days alone at Bullfrog Lake I didn't appear to do much. I let the world lead me. I've sometimes been asked if I contemplate nature or meditate when alone in the wilds. Both those sound too dynamic. They imply doing something. I'm not that active. I just let my mind wander where it will, picking up on hints and signs from the natural world. I don't try and direct my thoughts and sometimes I'm not aware of thinking at all. If something – a tree, a bird, a pattern in the snow – caught my eye I would watch it for a while until distracted by something else. No effort was involved and nothing really happened. Hours could pass without my being aware of them. I was absorbed in the world and not really aware of myself. I have been told this is meditation. If it is I did it without effort, thought or intention.

My companions returned the next morning bearing gifts of food and fuel and even a newspaper. The Onion Valley store had been closed so they'd gone out to the town of Independence in Owens Valley. Larry had brought me what seemed an enormous amount of food, all of it welcome. Half a loaf, a big chunk of cheese, a tube of honey, sugar, coffee, 12 instant puddings, 3lbs granola, 12 chocolate bars, 6 granola bars, 4 quarts of instant milk powder and 2.5lbs of trail mix ingredients. I needed the lot. My appetite was enormous. The crossing of the High Sierra was proving extremely strenuous and I had no fat reserves left. Every calorie I expended I needed to replace. I had a toasted cheese sandwich followed by honey sandwiches for lunch, which was a delicious change from the usual granola bars and trail mix. It was good to feel full too. Larry had also brought me up a quart of stove fuel, a pen, a lighter, a loo roll and, most precious of all, two rolls of film. I'd been rationing photos for several days. Now I could shoot a few more each day.

The day turned very windy and we had to repeg the tents more often. Larry's blew down twice – not that he was more careless than the rest of us but because the design meant it was more dependent on pegs for its shape. A raven flew into camp and scavenged some food scraps Andy and Phil had left, then hopped around just a few yards from the tents. Seeing one this close really brought home how big and magnificent these birds are.

In the evening we discussed plans. We were 12 days out from Kennedy Meadows but had only progressed 84 miles, partly due to the snow and partly due to the day on Mount Whitney and the days here. It was about 118 miles to Mammoth Lakes. We hoped to be there in ten days – and would be hungry if we weren't. We needed to speed up. The next day would see the end of my eighth week on the trail. Two months gone already. I'd planned on around 500 miles a month so should have walked about 1000. In fact it was just 650. Miles were needed.

Needed maybe. Gained no. The first day out from Bullfrog Lake we did just seven and a half miles in ten and a half hours. That did involve crossing 11,978 foot Glen Pass, which, along with Forester Pass, is the hardest and steepest in the High Sierra but even so it was disappointing. The approach to the pass was over hard snow so we needed crampons. The last section looked hard and dangerous with thin steep snow with lots of rocks and talus breaking through and nasty boulders at the bottom to hit if you slid back down. Deciding to avoid this we climbed safer looking slopes to a point about two hundred yards from the pass and then scrambled along the narrow rocky ridge to it. Real mountaineering again. Real mountain weather too with a piercingly cold wind. I needed gloves, balaclava, fibre-pile jacket and windproof jacket.

As with Forester the north side of Glen Pass was much gentler than the south, just a long wide snowfield. As the run-out at the bottom was just more snow we decided to glissade. This went well at first but then I caught my foot on something and flipped over twice, ending up with the pack pushing down on one shoulder. I couldn't get up without Scott's help. Once on my feet I decided to let the pack slide down on its own. This was a mistake. Initially it slid down smoothly but then it hit something, flew into the air and then burst open as it landed back on the hard snow, scattering my belongings over the snow where they then slid down the slope. With the

Storm approaching a camp in the High Sierra

assistance of the others my goods were eventually all retrieved and nothing was lost. Amazingly nothing was broken either except a pen that had snapped. I did lose some used guidebook pages, which blew away in the wind. At least being paper they would eventually rot away. I was most concerned about my camera gear but this was all okay, a credit to the heavily padded pouches I was using. Ironically, during the glissade a weld broke on Larry's external pack frame even though he'd had no problems with the descent. The broken frame was tied up with cord but clearly it wouldn't support the load as well and would have to be replaced once we were out of the mountains. Until then Larry would need to treat it carefully.

Beyond the glissade snowfield the terrain became steeper and more difficult so it took time to reach Rae Lakes. The views made up for the slow progress as we gazed on a ring of multi-textured, multi-coloured peaks at the head of the lakes, with Dragon Peak and Painted Lady standing out. The glorious landscape accompanied us to our campsite near Dollar Lake from where we had views of the great wall of Diamond Peak, the Rae Lakes peaks, the soaring tower of Fin Dome and jagged Mount Clarence King. It was an evening to sit outside and watch the mountains fade to silhouettes and a quarter moon shine in the sky.

Pondering mileage that evening I realised that worrying about it would only detract from the walk. I was here to enjoy being in wild places. Reaching the end of the trail was a convenient goal but it wasn't close enough to be concerned about yet. The walk was about the daily journey and the nightly camps not the final destination. Here in the snow I would go as far as I could each day and think about the next stage of the walk when it arrived.

Thinking this proved wise as we only progressed nine miles the next day and ten the following one. Continuing our descent from Dollar Lake we dropped below 9000 feet and below the snow for the first time in many days. The trail appeared, an actual footpath running through the woods, and led to a log bridge across the roaring snow-melt torrent of Woods Creek. Down here it felt like spring with birds singing, green shoots sprouting from the black sodden soil, still saturated with snowmelt, and many butterflies flitting about the sunlit meadows. The forest was richer than at timberline too with massive incense cedars, red firs and ponderosa pines plus aspens and willows beside the creeks. Being out of the snow and able to walk without crampons or snowshoes was a joy, albeit only a brief one as we were soon climbing back up 3,000 feet to camp on snow again at over 11,000 feet ready for the crossing of 12,100 foot Pinchot Pass. That evening thick white mist rolled in and blanketed our camp. For once we could see nothing. The mountains, our constant companions, had vanished.

The landscape reappeared for the climb to the pass. The early morning snow was hard and icy and we needed crampons. A long rising traverse across a steep snowfield with avalanche tracks

Snow travel in the High Sierra

down it, which made us glad we were here before the sun started to soften the snow, led to a final rocky scramble to the pass. The descent was easier than the ascent, something we were now coming to expect, and we were soon back down at timberline. Again the PCT dropped down into the forest before climbing back up. We decided not to do this however and instead stayed at timberline on a long and marvellous traverse above the glaciated canyon of the South Fork of the Kings River with the coloured bands of the metamorphic rocks of Striped Peak and Cardinal Peak always in view. In my journal I wrote 'superlative alpine scenery – as usual!' We camped in the Upper Basin of the South Fork ready for the next pass.

'A strange day ensued' starts my journal entry the next evening. So far we'd roughly followed the line of the PCT without any difficulties but now we went wrong. Looking up at the snow and rock wall above us, somewhere along which was 12,100 foot Mather Pass, we could see no sign of a trail. A notch in the ridge must be the pass we decided so we climbed up to it, at first on icy snow and then some final rock climbing that was unpleasant with crampons on. From the tiny narrow cleft we looked down on a lake that shouldn't have been there. This wasn't Mather Pass. Instead we were well to the east of it and some 400+ feet higher. How we'd made the mistake we couldn't work out. Luckily we didn't have to retreat but could descend the north side and rejoin the correct route at the frozen Palisade Lakes, down the centre of which we walked.

Below the lakes is a tight set of steep switchbacks blasted into the rock face known as the Golden Staircase. We certainly needed to be on the right route here as there was no other way down the steep rocks below the lakes basin. They were only partially snow-covered so following the switchbacks wasn't difficult. Then it was on down into the woods and out of the snow beside Palisade Creek. For the first time in over a week we camped on dry ground. At 8400 feet it was also the first camp below 9000 feet for two weeks and the first below 10,500 feet for a week. It was the last day of May and really spring-like. To save fuel we cooked over a wood fire. We also hung our food, something we hadn't bothered with up in the snow – and which wasn't possible at many high camps anyway as any trees were too small.

4000 feet of ascent led back up to 11,955 foot Muir Pass, the last time the PCT would be above 11,500 feet. Two mule deer, easy to identify due to the big ears that give them their name, watched us from the trees. Slowly the soft forest gave way to harder, rockier terrain. Glaciated granite walls and peaks rose all around. We crossed much avalanche debris and scrambled beside water slides on the Middle Fork of the Kings River. In places avalanches had swept right across the river and up the far side, tearing down big trees and scattering them like matchsticks. The thought of the force needed to do this was terrifying. Dramatic waterfalls poured down from the snowfields above. In a land of superlatives this day was especially spectacular, particularly magnificent LeConte Canyon with its vast slabs of smooth granite and unbroken rock walls.

Camp that night was the highest of the whole walk, at 11,600 feet above frozen Helen Lake, named for one of John Muir's daughters. The view back to the 14,000 foot summits of the Palisades was breath-taking. We were now in the heart of the John Muir Wilderness and it was an easy climb to Muir Pass itself. A beautiful octagonal stone hut marked the top. For once we could see no trees as the canyons either side twisted down between rock walls. The PCT runs for

John Muir Memorial Hut on Muir Pass, High Sierra
Larry at the camp below Muir Pass

ten miles above timberline here for the only time in the High Sierra. A big storm could be serious so far from the forest. Then the hut would be welcome.

As we descended from Muir Pass the highest section of the High Sierra was behind us but that didn't mean that all the difficulties were over. Nor the most beautiful and spectacular landscapes either. Indeed Evolution Basin, which lies below Muir Pass, is possibly the most impressive place on the PCT. A wide stony valley laced with lakes – Wanda, Sapphire and Evolution – and walled by granite peaks there is a feeling of mountain perfection here with every element of the scene balanced by every other.

Evolution Basin lies in the Evolution Group – Mounts Darwin, Mendel, Fiske, Haeckel, Huxley, Spencer, Wallace and Lamarck. The evolutionary names were given in 1895 by mountaineer and explorer Theodore S. Solomons who is important in the story of backpacking in the High Sierra as he was the first person to suggest and reconnoitre a trail the length of the range, an idea that eventually resulted in the John Muir Trail.

A gentle wander down Evolution Basin over the frozen lakes led to a steeper descent into the woods of Evolution Valley where we found the trail snow-free in places. It was an interesting game trying to follow the line of the trail through snow patches in the lodgepole pine forest. We hiked through a series of beautiful meadows before camping on the edge of one of them, Evolution Meadow. Again we cooked over a wood fire. I was becoming bored with my dried meals as was Larry with his so we mixed some of them together and added some spices to make something that tasted a bit different. It still had a familiar mushy texture though and I was beginning to look forward to fresh food with a bit of a bite to it. With maybe four days to Mammoth Lakes I could afford to start looking ahead. The longest section in the wilderness was approaching its end.

Dropping deeper into the forest we left most of the snow behind and were able to follow the trail easily as it ran beside the South Fork of the San Joaquin River. There were groves of aspen trees just coming into leaf and many flowers in the meadows, especially bright red paintbrush. The easy walk below soaring glaciated granite walls was a joy after all the hard going in the snow. I felt like a backpacker again rather than a mountaineer. We weren't finished with the snow yet though and the day ended with a climb back into it and a timberline camp at Sally Keyes Lakes. Here we met the first PCT hiker since Phil and Andy at Bullfrog Lake. Manuel had hiked the southern Sierra then dropped down into Owens Valley and walked the road before returning to the mountains. He had spare food which we gratefully received.

Now we were in slightly lower and mostly less steep terrain the nature of the challenges posed by the High Sierra changed. Our first taste of the new difficulties came after

Steep snow in the forest, High Sierra

Thawing lake in the High Sierra

we'd crossed lovely 10,800 foot Selden Pass and descended back into the forest. A ferocious creek barred our way. There was no bridge. In summer it was probably no more than a trickle. We ventured into the water and found it stronger and deeper – waist deep on me – than we'd expected. Dave somehow struggled across using his ski poles for support. Larry, Scott and I linked arms and only just made it. The snowmelt water was very cold and it took some time to warm up afterwards. I suspected there would be more of these fords to come as the snowmelt speeded up. That day other creeks were bridged though. Dipping in and out of the snow as the trail rose and fell we eventually dropped down to a low-seeming 7750 feet where we camped by Mono Creek. An almost full moon lit the forest. For the first time in ages I didn't pitch the tent but slept out under the trees.

The next fords came the next day. Larry and I were ahead of Scott and Dave now. We'd decided that when we reached the road we would try and hitch-hike into Mammoth Lakes and it seemed sensible to do this in pairs rather than as a foursome. A cold thigh-deep ford of the North Fork of Mono Creek was followed by a roped crossing of Silver Creek. We used the rope because there was a waterfall below the ford. I hadn't brought any rope but Larry had thirty feet, which was barely enough. I made a mental note to buy some more. After crossing Silver Pass – the passes now were easy compared with the rock notches to the south – we wandered through pleasant forests above Cascade Valley. Here I saw my first graceful mountain hemlock trees and in shaded places the strange red spikes of the parasitic chlorophyll lacking snow plant.

Late in the afternoon, for the first and only time in the High Sierra it snowed, flurries of big white flakes brought on a cold north-west wind. We took shelter in the gentle bowl of Tully Hole and squeezed the tents onto some snowfree ground below big trees. Mammoth Lakes was in reach so we no longer needed to ration food and ate large meals – pasta, instant soup, rice all mixed together and then instant puddings. None of it was satisfying though. I suspected this was because it was mostly processed carbohydrates, especially sugar. I wanted fats and protein to chew on and to fill me up.

With Mammoth Lakes so near I began to really look forward to a day or two in town. It was 25 days since, back in Weldon, I'd last had a shower, washed my clothes or eaten in a restaurant. Suddenly I really wanted to do all those. In the cold and the snow I hadn't noticed how dirty and smelly I was. Now, with temperatures staying above freezing, it became unpleasantly obvious.

The High Sierra didn't let us go without a final difficult day with hard going in soft and slippery snow to Duck Pass and then a nasty steep descent on icy snow. For the first time I needed to brake a fall with my ice axe. Finally though we emerged onto a highway. We'd crossed the snowbound High Sierra. Now it was time to get into town and celebrate. We stuck out our thumbs and soon had a ride. 'You look like you've been out some time', said the hikers who picked us up. 'Do you want to go to the campground or a restaurant first?' 'Restaurant' we responded instantly.

In Andersons Restaurant I ate a three-course meal with all trimmings, especially enjoying bread, cheese and crisp salad. It was huge and went down as if it was only a morsel. After this snack we made camp at the Shady Rest Campground. An hour after leaving we were back at the

Snow Plants

restaurant for another three-course meal. The waitress seemed surprised. Later in the evening Scott and Dave arrived. An ice cream parlour provided a pint of ice cream each to tide us over until morning.

After a shower the next morning I looked in the mirror at the bag of skin and bones that must be me. Only my legs had any muscle on them. My face was burnt dark despite all the glacier cream with pale circles round my eyes left by my sunglasses. My cheeks and chest were hollow, bones clearly visible. My arms were like matchsticks. Coming up was another long section, probably fifteen days, which meant another heavy load. I needed to replenish my energy as did the others so we spent two whole days in Mammoth Lakes, mostly eating. I collected my next food parcel plus mail and sat in restaurants writing letters and postcards. A bag of film went back to Kodak for processing. My pictures of the greatest adventure of my life so far.

A small ski and outdoor town Mammoth Lakes was an ideal place for such a long layover. Surrounded by forests and mountains I didn't feel I'd really left the wilds, more that I was resting on the edge. Not so big as to seem truly urban and city-like Mammoth Lakes was large enough to have outdoor stores and supermarkets so I was able to replenish my supplies and buy some necessary odds and ends such as new socks, mine all being in holes, a candle lantern (an unnecessary but tempting purchase – it wasn't actually much use) and 60 feet of 7mm rope. Larry bought a new pack to replace his broken one while Dave was lucky enough to meet a rep for The North Face who gave him a pack when he heard what he was doing. I sent my snowshoes to Warren Rogers – they were too big to mail home. I'd been carrying them much of the last few days and could do without the weight. My crampons, also seeing less use recently, did go home. I reckoned the snow would be soft and patchy enough from here on not to need them.

In Mammoth Lakes we saw Andy and Phil for the last time. They were going their separate ways, Andy to hitch-hike north in search of snowfree areas as he was sick of the snow and Phil to wait here, in his hometown, for the snow to melt. Other than Manuel we'd seen no other PCT hikers since Weldon and all sense of being part of a northbound backpacking community had vanished. Were any other hikers still on the trail? We didn't know.

Before leaving we weighed our packs in an outdoor store. I was shocked. Mine came in at 92lbs, Larry's went off the scale, which went up to 100lbs. We'd carried even more from Kennedy Meadows. How I didn't know but it certainly wasn't surprising that we'd only averaged 12 miles a day and that I'd eaten so much and still felt hungry.

A day in the woods from Mammoth Lakes saw us at Reds Meadow, a summer resort with various facilities. Now it was still snowbound and everything was closed. Hiking through sombre dark snowbound red fir forest we'd seen little. Tomorrow we'd return to the mountains. I lightened my load a little here as I discovered that my balaclava and long johns had shrunk in the drier at Mammoth Lakes, something I'd managed not to notice at the time. They went into a trash bin and I hoped forthcoming nights wouldn't be too cold.

Before leaving Reds Meadow we had a look at the Devil's Postpile, a strange hexagonal columnar basalt rock volcanic formation the same as the ones that make up the Giant's Causeway in Northern Ireland and Fingal's Cave on the island of Staffa in the Hebrides. It looked like nothing else we'd seen on the walk.

Beyond Reds Meadow a new difficulty arose. The snow formed suncups – a series of bowls separated by thin ridges. Walking on these was hard-going, especially when they were big enough to be more than a stride apart and deep enough to require a high step to exit. Geometric uniformity seemed the theme of the day with the regular columns of the Devil's Postpile and now the regular depressions of the suncups.

To make up for the hard work of the day we had a superb camp on a rocky bluff looking at Mount Ritter, Banner Peak and the pinnacles of the Minarets, fine mountains all. The first known ascent of the great rock block of Mount Ritter was by John Muir in 1872.

We were all struggling to adjust to being back in the snow with heavy packs. I think mentally we felt the success of the High Sierra crossing should mean being done with the snow and

In soft snow in Yosemite National Park

we were now beginning to resent it. Our third day out from Mammoth Lakes was, in the words of my journal, 'strange and frustrating'. I was in a daze at first and the others seemed no better off. Concentrating on finding the trail in the snow was beyond us and it took four long postholing, trail losing hours to reach 1000 Islands Lake, a rate of maybe a mile an hour. The only consolation was the superb view along the lake to the mountains. Soon though we were back in dark red fir forest, also known as snow forest as the shade of these giant conifers means the snow lasts longer here than elsewhere. From the lake we straggled up through soft snow to Island Pass then dropped down to a camp beside Rush Creek. We'd progressed just eight miles. So much for easier going on the lower terrain. None of us felt very cheerful.

By the next evening our spirits were much improved. We'd walked seventeen miles and had reached Tuolumne Meadows where the store had opened for the summer just two days before – it had been closed when we were in Mammoth Lakes so we'd made no plans to use it. This meant some fresh snacks that evening. We were also now in Yosemite National Park, pictures of which had been the original inspiration for my walk. Reaching Tuolumne Meadows had begun slowly with more difficult snow to deal with en route to 11,050 feet Donohue Pass, the last high pass on the PCT in the Sierra Nevada. It was on this pass that we entered Yosemite. To our great delight looking down from the pass we could see that long Lyell Canyon, which led to Tuolumne Meadows, was snow free. The last nine miles of the day down this beautiful springtime valley with its meandering creek took just three hours. We hadn't walked so fast since entering the High Sierra. The only downbeat note to the day was that my telephoto zoom lens had jammed with rust, having got damp on a creek ford. It never worked again.

Any idea that the most difficult and most dangerous part of the PCT was behind us was soon proved wrong in the Yosemite wilderness beyond Tuolumne Meadows. The next six days really were the toughest and most hazardous of the walk. The route here had the reputation for some of the steepest and longest ascents and descents on the PCT because it crosses the grain of the land, climbing over steep ridges and descending into deep canyons again and again, but these weren't really a problem after the High Sierra passes. However the route was also reputed to have some of the hardest creek crossings even in summer. Arriving at the height of the spring thaw with the creeks overflowing with snowmelt meant these fords would be really dangerous. Deep snow still lay in the high forests and on the passes too, making for much arduous postholing. Even the meadows were hard to cross as each was a mass of suncups, some of them several feet deep and several feet across. And to finish off the severity of Yosemite there were big thunderstorms nearly every afternoon. But it was the creeks I remember most vividly. So many creeks, so much water, so much noise, so much risk. Many years later I returned for a summer backpacking trip and found it hard to believe that the little creeks I could easily paddle or rock hop across were the same ones that had been so savage on the PCT.

From Tuolumne Meadows Larry and I travelled separately from Scott and Dave. This was a mistake. We'd gone through the High Sierra together so we could support each other, both practically and mentally. Now that we thought the going was getting easier we reckoned we

85

Clockwise: Larry on the trail, Tuolumne Meadows, Yosemite National Park
Lembert Dome, Tuolumne Meadows, Yosemite National Park
The Tuolumne River, Yosemite National Park

didn't need to do that. In fact this was just the time when being in a group would have been much safer.

Initially we followed a good trail beside the racing Tuolumne River, a wide deep torrent we wouldn't have considered fording. The amazing glaciated landscape around us was typically Yosemite with smooth rock domes and sharp spires – whale-backed Lembert Dome, the Horned Peaks of Unicorn and Cathedral, the big triangular face of Fairview Dome. Twice we crossed the river on bridges that were partly swamped by meltwater. At one some day-hikers – we met about twenty near Tuolumne Meadows, as many as on the rest of the walk so far put together – had paused and were staring at the water streaming over the bridge. They looked startled and somewhat shocked when we just stomped straight across. We didn't expect to keep our boots dry anyway. We passed the thunderous waterfall called White Cascade, the biggest we'd seen, before turning up Cold Canyon where we hit the first awful suncupped meadows and then a raging mass of water called McCabe Creek. Water crashed round the trees and surged over snowbanks, making it hard to tell which was creek and which land. Many fallen trees spanned the roaring water. We selected a group that looked secure and crawled gingerly across just inches above the boiling white-water. The noise was deafening and disorientating and the logs slippery and wet with sharp stubs. I found the crossing very frightening and was relieved to reach the sagging snow of the far bank.

Camp was in the forest but the night was still frosty. The air was humid from the melting snow and all this moisture vapour condensed and froze on the trees and our sleeping bags, turning them white. The rising sun soon dissolved the frost however. The ensuing day was long, hard, hot and slow. There were many creeks to cross. Two of them – Return Creek and Spiller Creek – were waist-deep and we roped up for safety, belaying each other from the bank. Whilst the ropes were psychological aids I doubt they'd have been much use and could even have been a hindrance if one of us had been washed away. But feeling that link with another person, along with using the tension of the rope to help with balance, made using it worthwhile. My sixty feet of rope was barely long enough, Larry's thirty feet wouldn't have been so I was glad I'd bought it.

The fords in freezing water left us shaky with cold. A steep arduous climb in soft deep snow soon warmed us up. The cold water seemed to have dulled our minds too as we made some map reading mistakes, lost the route and became completely confused. In the forest there were

Larry crossing McCabe Creek, Yosemite National Park

few landmarks so once we'd mislaid the trail finding it again was difficult. As we considered what to do Scott and Dave appeared, having followed our footsteps in the snow. Looking at the map we could see that Miller Lake, which lay beside the trail, should be easy to identify. Reluctantly we climbed up to a ridge so we could look down at the landscape. Miller Lake appeared below us so back down we went. On the trail again we were soon in spectacular Matterhorn Canyon, a wonderful glaciated valley rimmed with steep walls and laced with sparkling blue lakes and rich green meadows, many sodden but free of snow. Exhausted by the fords and the deep snow we camped after just seven miles. Since Mammoth Lakes I'd been sleeping out every night. Usually I was so tired I slept until dawn but in Matterhorn Canyon I woke in the dark and lay on my back staring up through a circle of trees at the stars shining in the totally clear black sky. I felt relaxed and in the right place. The travails of the day had gone.

More passes, more canyons and more fords marked the following day, along with being unsure of our whereabouts again. The fords were rough but didn't require roping up. The first pass, Benson, was just on timberline and gave grand views of surrounding peaks. Then it was back into the forest and down to Piute Creek. This stream had overflowed its banks and

Larry at a camp site in the Yosemite backcountry

spread out into the forest. If there was a bridge it wouldn't span most of the water. The area round the creek had become a swamp with many rotten fallen trees, mud and, a real nuisance for the first time, mosquitoes. The water was mostly slow but deep and we waded several waist-deep overflow channels before crossing the faster flowing main channel with another log crawl. Once out of the flooded forest we climbed through more magnificent glaciated scenery to Seavey Pass or at least somewhere near it. I wasn't convinced we'd reached the right spot. The next canyon, Kerrick, still lay below however so it didn't really matter. I just preferred knowing where I was. Scott and Dave decided to camp at the possible pass. Larry and I continued on, traversing steep but soft snow above yet another raging creek to camp about 100 feet above it amongst some red firs. The day again was hot, speeding up the snowmelt and leaving us sweaty but with cold wet feet from the wet snow.

Whenever there were views from passes and meadows we could see steep jagged mountains on the main Sierra Crest. This was the Sawtooth Ridge, the northernmost mountains in the Sierra Nevada over 12,000 feet high. Long before I knew about the PCT or wanted to visit the Sierra Nevada I'd read about these mountains as they appear in Jack Kerouac's novel *The Dharma*

Overleaf: Yosemite skyline

Flooded forest in Yosemite
Larry in Yosemite National Park

Bums, which describes his attempt on one of them, Matterhorn Peak, in the company of a group including Japhy Ryder, who is a lightly fictionalised version of the poet Gary Snyder. A real mountaineer and wilderness lover unlike Kerouac, who was really more at home in bars and cars, Snyder wrote several poems featuring this area of Yosemite, one of them called *Piute Creek*. Inspired by Snyder Kerouac did spend some time in the mountains and became entranced with the idea of backpacking and wild camping, writing in *The Dharma Bums* 'I wanted to get me a full pack complete with everything necessary to sleep, shelter, eat, cook, in fact a regular kitchen and bedroom right on my back, and go off somewhere and find perfect solitude'. This didn't last however, perhaps if it had Kerouac would have had a happier and longer life.

The three days since Tuolumne Meadows had felt dominated by water with much time spent on creek crossings. There was more to come however. My journal entry for the fourth day begins 'a day of water!' It started with a crossing of Kerrick Creek. This foaming torrent looked unfordable so we cast around for a logjam. And not far downstream from the trail we found a massive one where the whole forest on both banks had been avalanched with big trees thrown over the creek. We crossed on several solidly jammed logs, again inching along in a maelstrom of foam, surging waves and deafening noise.

Relief from the water and the snow came on an ascent of a rocky trail lined with flowers. Birds sang in the trees and a buck mule deer, his antlers in velvet, watched us from the forest. Soon though we were going down again to the next ford – Stubblefield Canyon Creek. To cross this very deep and fast creek we went upstream to where three creeks merged to form it and forded each one separately. One of these was chest deep and all were strong. We roped up for two of them.

Another snow-free ascent followed. We were becoming used to this pattern now. Up south-facing slopes where the snow had melted to a pass on a spur of the main crest then down in deep snow into a canyon where there were creeks to ford before the next ascent. The next descent took us to nearly ice-free Wilma Lake where we had a knee-deep wade to the bridge over the outlet. Jack Main Canyon Creek was a wide, deep river that we quickly decided was beyond our fording abilities even with the aid of the rope. Instead we would work our way along the bank until we found somewhere it seemed safer to cross. That night we stopped near the creek and had just lit a fire when a huge thunderstorm broke out with torrential hail the size of marbles followed by heavy rain. We pitched the tents extremely quickly but still had much damp gear – though some of this was from the fords. The storm raged through the evening then declined to mist and drizzle. I realised it was the first real storm for two months.

Morning came with cloud and dampness. We spent a whole day slogging up Jack Main Canyon through soft snow and collapsing suncups. I was becoming disenchanted with this section of the

Larry crossing Kerrick Creek, Yosemite National Park

trail. The effort required and the frightening fords seemed far in excess of the rewards. There was no choice but to go on anyway so I dismissed these thoughts. I certainly wasn't going back! My mood improved when the sun appeared and we started to dry out. Then we reached Tilden Creek, the ultimate ford. It took an hour and half. This was because it was so wild and fast and furious that we decided we needed a fixed line across it. Larry crossed first, without his pack but with the rope tied round his waist. Near the far bank the water knocked him over but he managed to scramble out. With the rope tied between two trees and attached to it by a karabiner linked to a belt made by wrapping his bear bagging cord round and round his waist Larry returned, collected his pack and took it to the other side. Then it was my turn. Larry weighed 12 stone and was over six feet tall and found the crossing difficult. At 10 stone and 5 foot eight inches I just swung from the karabiner edging along on my heels, the force of the waist deep water bending me double. We now had the problem of retrieving the rope. Neither of us wanted to cross without it being tied between the trees. Then Larry said he knew a knot that came undone when you pulled the cord attached to it but which was otherwise secure though he hadn't wanted to use it when carrying the packs. Back over the river he went to tie this knot and come back with the cord. Unfortunately just as he reached the bank he dropped the cord and away it went back to the far side. So Larry had to go back and start again. This time it worked. Larry had now forded Tilden Creek seven times. I was very impressed. Just once had been enough for me.

As if Tilden Creek wasn't enough shortly after the ford we were crossing big Grace Meadow when a thunderstorm broke above us and lightening cracked all around. We dashed for the trees, amazed at how fast we could run through sloppy snow with heavy packs when we were scared enough. Once secure in the forest we camped, after just seven miles. I'd felt tired all day and was now exhausted. Yosemite was proving tougher than I'd expected. We left the park the next day though at Dorothy Lake Pass. Looking ahead we were amazed and relieved to see that the mountains were mostly snow free. We were also delighted when we found a bridge over the West Fork of the West Walker River after descending from the pass. Although we didn't know it the hardest part of the walk from Mammoth Lakes to Echo Lake was over.

Yosemite was hard because of the steep glaciated terrain and the narrow canyons. On leaving the park the landscape changed dramatically. Gone were the steep cliffs and big rocky mountains,

Larry fording Tilden Creek

here the hills were lower and more rounded. The granite of Yosemite vanished. Here the volcanic rocks had a different colour, texture and form, which made for gentler more open scenery and easier walking. Steady rain that afternoon following another thunderstorm had me walking in my waterproof jacket for the first time on the walk. It had been worth bringing after all!

My appetite had not diminished and despite what had seemed like the enormous amount of food I'd carried from Mammoth Lakes, and which had been topped up at Tuolumne Meadows, I was running out again as was Larry. So when we reached Highway 108, the first since Tuolumne Meadows, we diverted from the trail and walked seven miles to Leavitt Meadows store where we found Scott and Dave who couldn't resist the thought of food either but who'd managed to hitch a lift. Here I stuffed myself with cheese sandwiches, soft drinks, fruit pies and coffee. It all tasted glorious. I then stocked up on candy bars and fruit pies for the next few days. Despite us spending quite a bit of money the store owner made it clear he didn't like backpackers and hassled us about packing up the groceries we'd bought outside the store. 'An unpleasant nasty man' I wrote in my journal. He stood out as the only person I met on the trail who was like that. His other customers were friendly however and interested in our walk.

Not wanting to walk back up the highway Larry and I joined Scott and Dave in hitch-hiking. It took three hours to get a ride but when we did the driver took all four of us and insisted on giving us fresh bread, cheese, butter and salad vegetables. His generosity more than made up for the crabby store owner.

Sonora Pass on Highway 108 is generally thought to mark the northern end of the High Sierra. From here on the Sierra Nevada is lower and less mountainous. The volcanic hills certainly looked different and the walking was easier, though in places there was still much snow, and mostly in the forest. Larry and I spent the first day north of Sonora Pass following Scott and Dave's tracks, relying on them not to lose the trail, and then joining them to camp. The walking was suddenly less committing with no high passes, deep fords or icy slopes to contend with and I was able to relax more and let my mind wander. The weather was worse though and again heavy rain, hail and thunder raged through the afternoon. I was glad we hadn't had such weather further south. The only real interest to the day was my first sighting of a porcupine, a large greenish beast that tried to climb a tree on seeing us but slid back down before wandering off into the trees, having seemingly forgotten our presence.

Midsummers Day arrived with mist and drizzle that dripped from the trees. The longest day remained damp as we slogged through thawing snow and along muddy trails below impressive purple, red, green and grey volcanic cliffs and pinnacles. The landscape felt more spread out and less mountainous. Here the forests dominated. The remoteness and sense of pristine wilderness had gone too. Sometimes we hiked on jeep tracks and highways appeared every so often. Following the trail wasn't always easy though as sections were still snow-covered and some junctions were unsigned. Four days out from Sonora Pass Larry and I became completely unsure of our whereabouts. We were trying to locate a seemingly distinctive hill called The Nipple. However the first hill we thought might be it wasn't and eventually we gave up trying to find it and just headed along a trail going roughly in the right direction. I was reminded of Alice in *Through the Looking Glass* only being able to reach a hill by walking away from it and was talking about this to Larry when we found a signpost. We were traversing The Nipple. Below us lay the half-frozen Blue Lakes just where they should be.

Larry following the trail through volcanic rocks in Northern California

Eleven miles remained to Echo Lake and the end of the second longest continuous section of the PCT. The 178 miles from Mammoth Lakes had taken 16 days. The marathon crossing of the High Sierra really was over now. It had been the toughest backpacking trip I'd ever undertaken yet also the most satisfying. The landscape had been the most spectacular I'd ever seen too. However I needed to increase my daily mileage if I was to have any chance of reaching Canada. In total I'd now walked 942 miles in 83 days, an average of only just over 11 miles a day. I hoped that easier terrain ahead would mean I could increase that greatly without too much effort.

Despite the need to press on I also needed a rest, as did Larry so we spent that afternoon and most of the next day at Little Norway, a hamlet above Echo Lake. Scott and Dave were going for a longer break and hitch-hiked to South Lake Tahoe. At Little Norway we slept in a woodshed and used the bar as an office and packing room. There was a PCT register in the Post Office from which we learned that Ken, who we'd last seen in Weldon and who'd planned on hiking up the highway in Owens Valley had been here three weeks ago, despite having ten days off in Independence with an infected blister on his foot. Clearly hiking the highway was much faster than traversing the snows of the High Sierra. I had no doubts about my preference though.

On learning we'd come through the High Sierra the Postmaster put us in contact with Mike Lewis, a reporter from the local paper, the North Lake Tahoe Bonanza, who wanted to interview

North Lake Tahoe Bonanza

the first PCT hikers to make it through the snow. We spent an evening with Mike in the bar and he said he'd send us copies of the interview. Sure enough several weeks later a photocopy of the article arrived in the mail. Mike described us as 'looking like miners out of an 1849 gold rush photograph' in the picture he took. We certainly looked rather wild and in my case very skinny. Two other PCT hikers turned up while we were at Little Norway. John was heading south and planning on finishing at Mount Whitney. He had discouraging tales of 50% snow cover ahead along with difficult fords and route finding problems. Our stories of Yosemite weren't encouraging for him either. After John had left the second PCT hiker turned up – by bus! This guy had started two weeks after me and had made it all the way to Tuolumne Meadows without any snow or ice gear. The Yosemite creeks had stopped him though. He'd fallen into Spiller Creek and trapped his foot between two rocks. Somehow he'd then managed to free himself and scramble out but with a sprained ankle and a badly gashed foot. With difficulty he'd limped back to Tuolumne Meadows where a doctor advised him he needed to take a few days or more off from hiking whilst his injuries healed. Not wanting to tackle the creeks again anyway he'd caught the bus to here. He'd been lucky to survive the creeks and very brave to tackle them on his own. There's no way I'd have done that.

Hoping for less snow and warmer weather ahead and liking the idea of lighter loads Larry and I both sent home some gear. I managed to shed 10lbs including the rope, Larry double that. With resupply points closer together now as well we'd be carrying much less, which should make hiking easier and also longer daily mileages more feasible. Although we both intended hiking solo eventually Larry and I decided to stay together until we were sure there were no more deep creek fords or big snowfields to deal with. Ahead lay the northern Sierra Nevada and then the start of the Cascade Mountains before we finally left California.

CHAPTER 3

OUT OF THE SIERRA INTO THE CASCADES: NORTHERN CALIFONIA

ECHO LAKE TO WRANGLE GAP

June 25 to July 31

599 miles

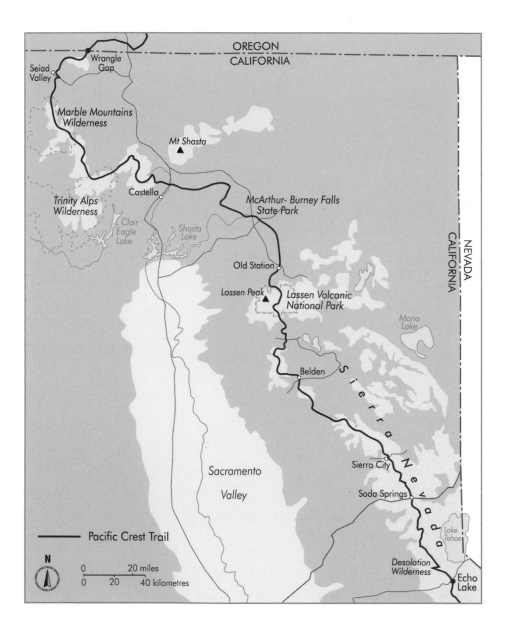

OREGON

CALIFORNIA

Wrangle Gap

Seiad Valley

Marble Mountains Wilderness

Mt Shasta

Trinity Alps Wilderness

Castella

Clair Eagle Lake

Shasta Lake

McArthur- Burney Falls State Park

Old Station

NEVADA

CALIFORNIA

Lassen Peak

Lassen Volcanic National Park

Mono Lake

Belden

Sierra Nevada

Sacramento Valley

Sierra City

Soda Springs

Lake Tahoe

Pacific Crest Trail

N

0   20 miles

0   20   40 kilometres

Desolation Wilderness

Echo Lake

Susie Lake, Desolation Wilderness

The walk through Northern California would see a wide variety of scenery and more roads and towns than I was used to encountering, along with too much logging and the desolation of clear-cut forests. Much of the walking was in forest on fairly level trails which, combined with much lighter loads, meant that, as I'd hoped, my daily mileage increased without much extra effort or longer days. Larry and I didn't leave Little Norway until late afternoon however so our first day was just five and a half miles. This took us into the Desolation Wilderness, whose name sounded forbidding but was contradicted by the beauty of the landscape. Apparently it's named for the amount of bare rock and the thinness of the forest. These of course make it attractive for wilderness lovers and hikers and it's a very popular summer backpacking area.

Desolation Wilderness was all water and rock with scattered trees. Lakes were everywhere, still half-frozen and shining in the sunlight. The first night we camped above Margery Lake and then passed Lakes Aloha, Heather and Susie the next morning. Above them rose rugged Pyramid Peak

101

and the summits of the Crystal Range, lower mountains than those of the High Sierra but still impressive. There was still plenty of snow on the ground but there was now much more wildlife than we'd seen further south with marmots, chipmunks and squirrels common. Then we climbed to the last point above 9,000 feet on the PCT, 9380 foot Dicks Pass, before descending to pass yet more lakes – Dicks, Fontanillis, Upper Velma and Middle Velma – and then camping in the forest.

Fifteen miles had passed without much effort. The next day we walked twenty-two which, I wrote in my journal, 'seemed no effort either'. Most of the time we were in pleasant forest with few views. The trail was fairly level so there was no reason not to stride out. After the High Sierra and 900 miles of walking we were very fit. There were plenty of PCT markers on trees too so we didn't often have to spend time looking for the trail. These markers were inconsistent – common in some places, non-existent in others. That night we camped at 6200 feet, the lowest since Kennedy Meadows, 46 long days ago.

Desolation Wilderness was left for a stretch of 'non-wilderness' forest, which means it can be used for logging and other uses, though we didn't notice any difference this time and soon we were in what is now the Granite Chief Wilderness and back then had the rather cumbersome bureaucratic name Granite Chief Motor Vehicle Closure Area. Here I regretted sending the rope home when we were faced with a ford of the deep and fast North Fork of the American River. Scouting up and down the bank we eventually found a point where it split into two channels, one of which we waded while the other was crossed with a log crawl – a rather tame one compared with those in Yosemite but still exciting enough.

Leaving Granite Chief – we were to become used to rapid changes in land designations and usage in Northern California, the wilderness areas here were much smaller than in the High Sierra and generally not contiguous – we went through a stretch of private property with many threatening no trespassing, keep out and private notices. Ignoring these but feeling it might be wise to be out of sight we camped in a dense stand of firs a few hundred yards from the PCT, which at this point was a dirt road.

During the day I finally identified two big flowering plants we'd seen grow from little shoots to big plants in the last few weeks. The very green thick-leaved bulky ones with spikes of white star-like flowers that were now two feet high and more were corn lilies (though no relation to actual lilies), the aromatic yellow sunflower-like ones were mountain mule's ears (which is a member of the sunflower family). The first grew in profusion in damp meadows, the latter on dry stony slopes. Both were to be regular companions in coming weeks.

So far my gear had held up well. However on

Mountain Mule's Ear

feeling rubbing in my boots I examined them and noticed that the linings were disintegrating. The soles were losing their tread too. I'd been wearing them almost all the time since we reached the Sierra Nevada because of the snow. I had thought I'd have them resoled. Now I thought I'd replace them with lighter footwear more like my running shoes. I was looking forward to hiking in the latter when we finally escaped the snow but I knew they too wouldn't last much longer.

Heavy rain fell on our 'private property' camp and we woke to thick mist drifting through the trees. We were certainly well-hidden. The rain continued all the way to little Soda Springs where we arrived soon after the post office opened, following an early start. Here I collected the smallest food parcel of the walk, just three days' worth. The Cheese Store Deli provided an excellent second breakfast of an omelette (I really missed eggs on the trail) and coffee plus snacks for the next few days. Soda Springs also had a laundromat, which was sorely needed as it was the first since Mammoth Lakes, now a long sweaty and arduous three weeks behind us. There was a PCT register in the post office full of entries from hikers who'd skipped round the snow and started again from here. Not that they had missed the snow, there was still plenty in the woods, but they had missed the combination of snow and steep mountains and remoteness and with it the glorious High Sierra. Soda Springs was also significant because on reaching it I'd now hiked 1000 miles. At least it felt significant.

Soda Springs lies not far from the notorious Donner Pass, the one pass in the Sierra Nevada widely known in the outside world due to the tragedy that overtook the Donner Party here in 1846. These pioneers were trying to cross the mountains to the rich lowlands of western California but were trapped here by deep snow in the autumn. Rescuers tried to reach the party but did not do so until February, by which time 39 people were dead, leaving 48 survivors. Now the 7200 foot gentle pass is crossed by a railroad and an Interstate highway and it's hard to imagine how such a disaster could have happened. It's still often closed by blizzards in the winter though.

With rain still falling and the mist still thick we left Soda Springs in late afternoon to walk through snow for a few miles to the Sierra Club's Peter Grubb Hut, which was like a large Scottish bothy (unlocked shelter with few facilities beyond a roof). The hut was built in 1938-39 as a memorial to Peter Grubb who died on a cycling tour of Europe and is one of the few such shelters on the PCT. It was basic but dry inside and had a large fireplace. As it was so wet outside we decided to stay and soon had a big fire going that raised the temperature to 18°C and quickly dried out our damp gear. This proved very useful as the wet weather continued. At least our gear could begin getting damp again rather than get even damper. We woke to thick mist and one of those days that thankfully is soon forgotten. 'Another wet, wet day' I wrote in my journal after hours of slogging through melting snow in the dripping forest. Where the trail wasn't snow-covered it was thick with ankle-deep mud. A break in the drizzle came at noon when the heavens opened and we were assaulted by torrential rain, hail, thunder and lightning. Rushing along heads down in our waterproofs we just wanted to make as many miles as possible. Stopping to camp in this didn't seem attractive anyway. Finally we ran out of energy and made a damp camp in thick mist and steady rain. This dismal dark weather continued all the following day when we walked 19 miles 'on sodden jeep roads through sodden forest' to Sierra City (population 225), an old gold mining town in the North Yuba river canyon that now relies on tourism for its main business. The only enjoyable part of the day was the final descent down steep switchbacks into an area of magnificent trees – black oaks, maples, Douglas firs and ponderosa pines. Although we were making good progress the sense of excitement and adventure we'd felt in the High Sierra and Yosemite had gone. The challenge here was simply to keep going, to keep walking through the mist and rain.

Having pitched our wet tents at the Wild Plum Campground we went into Sierra City to collect mail and supplies. Here our luck changed. In the store a man guessed we were PCT hikers and offered to let us stay in his house, something he did regularly for thru-hikers. Bob Frost was a Forest Service Fire Prevention Technician who lived just outside Sierra City. His generosity meant we were able to dry out our gear again and take showers – the first for 23 days, since Mammoth Lakes in fact. I expect we needed them!

Rising above Sierra City and the North Yuba River are the rock towers and pinnacles of Sierra Buttes, one of the highest and most distinctive peaks in the northern Sierra Nevada. (It's 8591 feet – how the mountains had dwindled since the High Sierra!). The mist had kept Sierra Buttes hidden on the descent to Sierra City but it came into view during the steep and brutal ascent from the North Yuba river canyon and the following traverse round steep scrub-covered slopes. Whilst the summits were impressive the mountainside we crossed had been heavily logged, which somewhat detracted from the wild feel. For the last time we lost our way for a while in an area of confusing partly snow-covered logging roads before PCT waymarks appeared again.

The mix of logging roads and foot trails in clear-cut areas and healthy looking forest, probably second growth, continued for the last 85 miles of the Sierra Nevada. Much of the time we were hiking in red fir forest with few views. The going was mostly good though, with little snow left, and we made over 20 miles a day. At times we could see ahead to the first peaks of the Cascades – the white cone of Mount Shasta, which would be a dominant feature for the next weeks, and the summit of Lassen Peak – which drew us on with the promise of more spectacular landscapes ahead. The weather improved, which helped morale a good deal, and it was hot in the forest. For the first time on the walk I ended days with sore feet, a combination of the extra miles we were hiking, the hard-packed ground and over-heating in my big boots, which I was still wearing for the sections of snow. Fine in deep snow all day these boots were too hot now we'd returned to summer trail backpacking. On one day the temperature at 1 pm was 22°C in the shade.

Whilst the general landscapes were no more than pleasant the sections of unspoilt forest were often magnificent with big incense cedars, white firs, silver pines, red firs, ponderosa pines and Douglas firs. The flowers were wonderful too – red paintbrush and purple lupins joining the yellow mountain mule's ears. The trail followed the dry crest of the hills for long distances and for the first time in many weeks we had to carry water. These hills were rolling, green and forested – a far cry from the rugged mountains of the High Sierra, whose snowy peaks we could see far to the south at times.

One steep descent led down to Franklin Canyon and the Middle Fork of the Feather River, across which we were pleased to see a graceful bridge. Other creeks and rivers were bridged too so we had no more difficult fords. Larry had brought some lightweight fishing gear and tried fishing in some of these waters but without any luck.

Approaching Belden and the end of the Sierra Nevada the scenery improved as we hiked through what is now the Bucks Lake Wilderness. The PCT ran along the rim of a valley with views over a lake-dotted forest and then descended gradually over ground covered with attractive tough red-barked manzanita bushes. Ahead were views across the deep North Fork of the Feather River valley to the first hills of the Cascades. The final descent to Belden and the North Fork was a leg-hammering steep six miles down 36 switchbacks through dense undergrowth that was head high in places. The guidebook warned of poison oak but I somehow managed to avoid brushing against this innocuous looking but poisonous plant which I only learned to identify from warning notices in the campground that evening.

Belden was a tiny hamlet (population 22) but had a combination post office/store/café and bar plus a campground. As well as my food parcel I had eight letters from home, which were very welcome, and a copy of the North Lake Tahoe Bonanza with the interview with me and Larry in it. I read this with interest and noted in my journal that it was 'very flattering if not quite accurate'. In the trail register were entries from over 20 PCT hikers who'd skipped the High Sierra and bussed round from Weldon. The next day one more snow-avoiding PCT hiker arrived. Mark had made it from Campo to Yosemite, where he'd waited for two weeks before catching the bus here as there was still more snow than he wanted to deal with.

At 2300 feet Belden was the second lowest camp of the walk so far, only Cabazon had been lower, away back in the California desert. Like Sierra City Belden was in a narrow steep-sided pass that took roads and railways through the mountains and out of which we had to climb.

Larry fishing in Squaw Valley Creek
Poison Oak

Although the landscape looked much the same we were finally leaving the Sierra Nevada and entering the Cascade Range, which we'd follow all the way to Canada. The Cascades stretch for 700 miles in a straight line and are characterised by big isolated volcanoes surrounded by lower non-volcanic gentler hills. In the North Cascades the range becomes more rugged and alpine. It would be many weeks before I'd reach those spectacular mountains.

As well as increasing my appetite was producing some strange cravings, particularly for tinned mandarin oranges, not something I normally eat so why I suddenly desired them I had no idea. Whenever they were available I ate them. I also longed for eggs, which wasn't so surprising – my trail diet was low in protein and I liked them anyway. Of course I could have carried both but they were heavy and in the case of eggs breakable. My cravings weren't so strong that I was prepared to carry the extra weight. At Belden I indulged them by breakfasting on three soft-boiled eggs followed by a tin of mandarins in camp. A second breakfast of microwaved sandwiches and coffee at the store set me up for the long and steep 4,500 foot climb out of the North Fork of the Feather River gorge. From the switchbacks we could look back down to the narrow canyon with its crammed-in road, railway and reservoir. There was more poison oak on the trail and a glorious succession of trees from black oaks and ponderosa pine low down through incense

107

The Cascade Mountains in Northern California

cedars, white firs, sugar pines and finally dense and sombre red firs. I was coming to realise that the real glories of Northern California lay in the trees rather than the mountains.

Now there was little snow left on the trail Larry and I discussed going on our own ways, which meant I could leave later in the morning and walk later in the evening and Larry could do the opposite. We'd become good friends and had happily accommodated each other's foibles but I was becoming restless and wanted to be alone again so I was free to vary my routine and follow any whims such as making camp at lunchtime by a pleasant lake or hiking into the night. However the first night out from Belden Larry's stove caught fire with a dramatic flare-up that melted the edge of his tent flysheet but luckily didn't set anything on fire. The next morning the now cool stove still leaked fuel and so was unsafe to use. For the next week we'd stay together and cook on my stove, which was still working fine.

Once the climb from Belden was over the walking was easy on good trails in gentle forest. Every so often the rapidly approaching Lassen peaks would appear and in open sections we could see crags and pinnacles above us. For the first time we met a trail crew opening the trail by sawing up blown-down trees and checking blazes. In forested areas this is a necessary task every year once the snow has gone. We'd got used to clambering over or round the occasional tree across the trail but horse packers use these trails too and need them clear.

For the first time we also met PCT hikers who were heading south. These two had hiked from Campo to Weldon then travelled up to Ashland in Southern Oregon and were now heading south back to Weldon. They then intended going to the northern terminus of the PCT at Manning Park in Canada and hiking south to Ashland, which meant we might meet up again (we didn't). That way they should manage to hike the whole trail without having to deal with snow. This approach was practical but didn't appeal to me. I had a simple view of a long walk. Begin at the beginning and walk to the end. I wanted it to be a continuous journey, broken only by going out occasionally for supplies, after which I would always return to the point at which I'd left the trail. 'Hike your own hike' is a popular long-distance hiker saying, which I agree with so I wouldn't criticise anyone's way of hiking but doing a long walk in sections in different directions isn't for me.

The two PCT hikers (one was called Mark, the other's name I neglected to note) had other information on the year's trailers, reminding Larry and me that we weren't actually alone on the trail. They said that many people had given up, including some of those we'd met in Southern California, and that the Forest Service had issued 120 PCT thru-hiker permits by April 23rd when they'd set off. Many years later I learned that according to the PCTA only 11 people finished the trail (which included me, Larry and Scott) so the drop-out rate was very high, mainly, I think, due to the late deep snow in the Sierra Nevada.

Not far out of Belden we entered the Lassen National Forest and the best waymarked trails we'd yet encountered. There were plenty of blazes and PCT diamond markers on the trees and every junction was signed with mileage figures as well as directions. So when we reached the popular Domingo Springs Campground, where we stayed because it had water, which was rare in this section, we knew we were 53 miles from Belden and had walked 21 miles that day, assuming of course that the figures were accurate (the guidebook made the distances 5 miles longer). These signs made the walking much quicker as we never had to stop to check maps or the guidebook. They also made the walk less challenging of course and I wouldn't have liked much of the trail to be like this. In fact searching for the trail in the snow and learning how to work out where it went had been interesting and enjoyable even if it did take time. Larry and I had become quite good at seeing the line of the hidden trail through the trees and spotting the occasional faded old blaze. But for now rapid progress on well-marked trails was a pleasant change.

Three days out of Belden we reached Lassen Volcanic National Park, the first national park since Yosemite. 10,457 foot Lassen Peak is the centre of the park and the southernmost of the Cascade volcanoes. It's not typical though, being much less dramatic in appearance than the others. This is because it's the only Cascade volcano that isn't a stratovolcano, which is one made up of layers and layers of lava and other volcanic material built-up over long periods of geological time, a process that gives rise to the classic cone-shaped volcano, of which Mount Shasta is a good example. Lassen Peak however is a single plug of lava that was formed in a single eruption. It's the largest plug dome volcano in the Cascades – the only one above 10,000 feet in height – and one of the largest in the world.

The area is still active – the last eruption was in 1915 – and there were many volcanic features that I was looking forward to seeing as I'd never been to such a place before. Our entry to the park wasn't conducive to looking at the landscape though as it was in a cloud of mosquitoes, the worst on the walk so far. I was bitten many times before I managed to soak myself in repellent. Happily the bugs faded away as the sun grew stronger and the day became hotter and drier.

The first sign of vulcanism was a strong smell of rotten eggs from hydrogen sulphide drifting through the trees. Soon we came upon the series of yellow sulphur-encrusted fumaroles (vents) gushing hot water and clouds of steam that made up Terminal Geyser. Then came blue-green milky Boiling Springs Lake steaming gently in the sunshine, its water at a constant 52°C, and surrounded by small smoking fumaroles and bubbling mud pots slurping away noisily. Although we saw no more volcanic activity like this it stayed in my mind and I was aware throughout the rest of the walk that this was a volcanic region and that the earth was dynamic and mobile not far below our feet.

Beyond these fascinating volcanic features we traversed the park in fir and pine forest past several lakes before camping by Silver Lake. Unfortunately water meant mosquitoes and we

Boiling Springs Lake, Lassen Volcanic National Park
Terminal Geyser, Lassen Volcanic National Park

quickly retreated to our tents and lay inside listening to frogs croaking. Next day the walking continued through mosquito ridden woods past pale early morning lakes and out of Lassen Volcanic National Park (it's not a big park and the PCT is only in it for about 17 miles). From a ridge we had a grand view back to Lassen Peak. With this volcano behind us we were now truly in the Cascades.

Once out of the protected park lands the trail became a dirt road and we soon reached Old Station, the next supply town. It was now 33 days since we'd last had a day off from hiking so we decided to stay here for a day on the pleasant Hat Creek Campground where we camped in the shade of some superb ponderosa pines. We also planned on hitch-hiking to the much bigger town of Burney some seven miles away in the hope that stores there could provide a new safety valve for Larry's stove and some lightweight footwear for me – I really needed these now as both my boots and running shoes were disintegrating. Neither had much tread left, which was okay on gentle forest trails and dirt roads but wouldn't be on any steeper rockier terrain, especially if wet. We spent two hours the next day waiting for a ride – we could have walked there in that time. Burney had socks, books and a Safeways supermarket but no outdoor store so no stove valve or footwear.

Outdoor shower under a ponderosa pine at the Hat Creek campground
Burney Falls

From Old Station the PCT runs along the bare and waterless Hat Creek Rim for 30 miles. We were advised, both locally and by Warren Rogers, not to attempt this but to hike the highway instead. In retrospect I wished I'd carried the several gallons of water I'd have needed and stayed on the PCT. The highway was hell and we spent two days on it. At the end of the first one I wrote in my journal 'a long, hot, dusty tarmac plodding 86°F day. 16 miles of eternity! I'd rather tackle snow and flooded rivers'. The only point of interest was Subway Cave, a fascinating third of a mile long tube bored out of the rock by hot lava. Otherwise we progressed from café to café with a stop at a laundromat in which I sat in my waterproof trousers so everything else could be washed. I read most of the way along the road – Charles Dickens' *Dombey and Son* and Agatha Christie's *The Body In The Library*, the only books of interest I'd found in Burney. I wanted natural history guides and books on the Cascades but there had been none.

For once I carried a few tins a short distance for the evening meal – mushroom soup, cheese ravioli, strawberries – which made a nice change from dried stuff. To add to the discomfort of the road walk, which had left me with sore feet and one big blister, the night was full of mosquitoes, necessitating sealing myself into the tent where it was then uncomfortably hot (never below 16°C). I lay sweatily on my sleeping bag and didn't sleep well. A second to-be-

A viewpoint in Northern California with Mount Shasta

quickly-forgotten day on the road and we reached McArthur-Burney Falls State Park where we rejoined the PCT. The park store sold me a natural history guide to the Cascades and for fifty cents we were allowed to camp in the picnic area where we were joined by another PCT hiker, Susie, who was doing the section from Lassen Volcanic National Park to Canada. Not far away was Burney Falls itself, an impressive spring-fed 129-foot waterfall. A sign said that in the summer the river above the falls dries up and water spouting through holes in the rocks is all that feeds the falls but this early in the season both river and springs were flowing strongly.

Five mixed mostly forest walking days led to the next town, Castella in Castle Crags State Park, where Larry and I finally went our separate ways. For the first two days the mix of unsightly logged forest and fine untouched forest continued with much of the walking on logging roads with too many huge logging trucks roaring along them in clouds of dust and diesel. There were cows grazing in this multi-use forest too. With little snow anymore I wore my running shoes without socks as it was very hot, which meant I had to remember to apply insect repellent to my ankles as well as my face, arms and hands because mosquitoes appeared quickly in shaded areas, especially near water. As I'd discovered back in the desert at the start of the walk when it was hot my boots were more comfortable on my back than on my feet.

At times we hiked on thin trails above steep volcanic scree slopes with views of Mount Shasta, which towered some 10,000 feet above the surrounding green forested hills. This 14,179 foot volcano is the second highest summit in the Cascades and the most southerly of the line of stratovolcanoes that stretches the length of the range as well as one of the largest stratovolcanoes in the world. Its beautiful white-capped cone would be visible and eye-catching for many days. John Muir and a companion were once caught in a severe blizzard on the slopes of the mountain after a spring ascent and survived the night lying by some hot springs where they were alternately too hot or frozen (Muir had wanted to continue the descent, it was his companion who insisted on staying by the springs. His account can now be found online – http://www.sierraclub.org/john_muir_exhibit/writings/snow_storm_on_mount_shasta.aspx).

Camps in this section were all in the forest but that didn't mean finding suitable sites was always easy. Often the trail traversed steep ground with no suitable terrain at all. Twice we pitched our tents on the trail itself as it was the only flat ground available. We just hoped bears didn't use the trail during the night – we were seeing bear droppings regularly. At dubious intersections we left arrows in the dirt and little cairns for Susie, who was somewhere behind us. Just once she caught us up and we camped together and she showed us a beautiful obsidian Native American spearhead she'd found on the trail. To counter the mosquitoes she was taking vitamin B12 and Brewer's Yeast tablets, which she said had some effect. I was putting plenty of fresh garlic in meals as it was also supposed to repel mosquitoes. I didn't notice it making any difference but it did make the meals taste better. We never saw Susie again after this one camp and I never heard if she reached Canada.

Often the trail ran through open meadows and across dry, dusty hillsides replete with lovely flowers and with excellent views of the surrounding hills and the already very familiar cone of Mount Shasta. Altitude changes were mostly small but there was one seemingly endless, hot, twisting, foot-hammering, fly-ridden descent down to the McCloud River at just 2,600 feet. This descent actually took three hours and left both Larry and me with aching feet and legs. Relief was provided by a friendly family, who were car camping near the river, and who plied us with chili beans and beer.

The highlight of these hot dusty days was my first ever sighting of bears in the wild. On hearing a sound in the meadow above us we looked up and there just fifty or so feet away was a light brown bear (all the bears this far south are black bears but that doesn't

Mount Shasta

mean they are black or even dark) with two cubs feeding on berries, of which there were many – raspberries, blackberries, red currants and gooseberries. When one of the cubs started to move down the hillside towards us the mother stood up to get a better look at us. Remembering stories of she-bears defending their cubs we walked on briskly. I was excited and pleased at finally seeing a bear. It seemed an essential part of a PCT hike. They weren't reputed to be a problem here though and I hadn't hung my food since leaving Yosemite.

Later the same day we were molested by wildlife however – in the form of butterflies! We'd stopped for a snack beside a small stream in a deep gully when a cloud of black and white butterflies with orange tipped wings (called, I learnt later, Sara's orangetip butterflies) appeared and flew all around us landing on our arms, shoulders, backs, legs and packs. The air was filled with fluttering wings and I found this a strange and magical experience. There was probably a prosaic reason for it, like salt in our sweat, and if they'd been flies we'd have hated it but because they were so beautiful and delicate it felt very special.

A final hot waterless day with excellent views of Mount Shasta again and ahead to the massive ramparts of jagged Castle Crags took us to Castella and the Castle Crags State Park in a crowded valley with the Southern Pacific Railroad, Interstate 5, local roads and the Sacramento River all crammed in side by side. At the post office we found a note from Scott and Dave to say they had hitch-hiked here from Burney to avoid the last less interesting section of the trail as they now hadn't enough time left to finish the whole trail due to commitments in the autumn. So they were ahead of us now. The note went on to say that when they reached the next supply point at Seiad Valley they were going to hitch-hike again to Crater Lake in Oregon. I didn't expect to catch them up. They also said that their stove had actually exploded! Larry wasn't the only one to have problems. As we were all using the same model of stove I decided I'd better buy spares for my so far trouble-free one.

We also met a hiker here who'd we'd met on and off several times since the Mohave Desert crossing. He was always in town ahead of us and usually said he knew direct routes he'd learnt from rangers. Only once did we meet him on the trail though. He didn't look as though he'd been hiking for months, his leg muscles just weren't hard enough and he didn't have the skinny, famished look of a thru-hiker. His stories didn't ring true either and I found him rather irritating. We didn't want an argument so we didn't express our thoughts but just tried to ignore him.

Larry crossing a remnant snow patch with Mount Shasta on the horizon

Maybe he did know those 'secret' (his words) routes, maybe he had hiked the whole way. I found that hard to believe though. Of all the PCT hikers I met he was the only one whose stories didn't ring true and listening to them made me uncomfortable. I was later to hear from people who saw him hitch-hiking. Now skipping sections of the trail due to pressures of time or the snow or because you think they'll be dull is fine if that's what someone wants to do but pretending to have hiked a trail seems pointless as well as dishonest. After all, the person who really knows is yourself.

Although it was only a week since the last day off from the trail at Old Station I took another here as a local man we met offered to drive us to the town of Mount Shasta where he said there was an outdoor store. This was an opportunity not to be missed. With a population of over 3,000 Mount Shasta seemed enormous. I felt a little overwhelmed on the busy, noisy streets. I hadn't been anywhere this big for several months. There was indeed an outdoor store, The Fifth Season mountain shop, and it was excellent. After much deliberation and against the advice of the staff who couldn't believe I was going to try and hike 1200 miles in them I bought a pair of lightweight trail shoes, which was a new concept in hiking footwear in 1982. I was not yet totally convinced this was a good idea – in my journal I wrote 'I hope this is sensible!' Throwing caution to the winds I sent home both boots and running shoes.

There were other purchases too. Larry was very pleased at being able to buy a fuel cap for his stove. I bought one too, just in case. Other additions to my load were a tiny guide to Pacific Coast trees and a rather heavier guide to the birds of the Western USA plus a couple of novels. The most expensive items was a camera lens. Since ruining my 75-150 zoom lens during a creek ford in the High Sierra I had been left with just a 28mm wide angle lens, which was fine for big spreading landscapes but rather limited for some other shots. (Why I'd only taken those two lenses I don't know now, presumably to save weight). In Mount Shasta I found a photographic store and bought a 50mm lens, which would be good for close-ups of flowers, self-portraits and other pictures where the 28mm wasn't ideal. It also meant I had two lenses in case I wrecked another one.

At Castella Larry and I finally parted. It was nearly three months since I'd hiked alone and I was looking forward to the solitude and the freedom to make decisions as and when I chose. I now had 1200 or so miles to myself. Unsurprisingly my first decision was to have a leisurely breakfast while Larry's was to set off within minutes of waking up. My pack was heavy as it was 160 miles to Seiad Valley so I was carrying ten days supplies, though I hoped it would take less time than that (it took eight days in fact). The PCT makes a huge loop westwards here, leaving the Cascades for the Klamath Mountains, before returning back east. From the map it would seem more logical just to head north and cut the distance. But long distance-hiking isn't about logical routes, it's about the best routes, which means the most scenic, adventurous, challenging and exciting, and the Castella to Seiad Valley section went through the most impressive mountain landscapes since the High Sierra. There were magnificent forests too and two wilderness areas (four now, two having been designated since my walk). However there were also logged areas and rather too many ugly road scars. Wilderness here felt constrained some of the time.

As was now usual when leaving supply points there was a steep climb to start with, this time up 4,000 feet, an ascent mitigated by superb views of the huge cliffs and sharp spires of Castle Crags, now the centrepiece of the Castle Crags Wilderness Area. The trail was often in low chaparral- type bushes rather than forest, which was great for the views but not for shade from the hot sun. At one point a big green rattlesnake lying on the trail gave me a fright when I suddenly spotted it not far ahead. I hadn't seen one since the desert and had forgotten all about them. This snake didn't rattle but just crawled slowly away while keeping an eye on me.

Castle Crags

I quickly adjusted to being on my own, relishing going at my own pace, stopping when I wanted and camping when and where I liked. I also started to see more wildlife and soon realised just how much more disturbance is caused by two people compared with one. Mule deer were common, some with fauns, and I saw another bear, further away this time, and many birds, only some of which I could identify. Less pleasant were the nasty biting flies that became increasingly common. The dry terrain meant there were few mosquitoes but also not many creeks so I had to carry water some of the time. Although walking alone I did meet other people both on the trail and at camp sites as the summer hiking season was now in full swing.

I was also soon very pleased with my new footwear, the shoes proving much cooler than the boots whilst giving more support than the running shoes. I also felt more secure now I had footwear that wasn't falling apart. However other equipment was beginning to show signs of wear. My clothes had many holes in, especially my shorts, but most serious was a problem with my pack. I'd noticed since Castella that it seemed to press on one hip and felt unbalanced. I thought I must have packed it badly but on examining it one evening I discovered that the internal metal frame had snapped at one corner so that side was less supportive than the other. The frame was bolted and sewn-in, making removal difficult, and the pack was a British make so I doubted I could have the frame replaced here. It looked like I needed a new pack, an expense I could do without. That would have to wait until I found another outdoor store though. In the meantime I had to manage with the discomfort. I remembered the pack bouncing and bursting open as it slid down Glen Pass back in the High Sierra. The frame had probably been weakened then. Just to add to my annoyance I also discovered I'd lost my Swiss Army Knife.

Mount Shasta still dominated the views though I was now heading away from it towards the peaks of the Trinity Alps and the Marble Mountains. The PCT cuts through a corner of the first and then spends rather more time in the second. These would be the first wilderness areas for quite a while and I was looking forward to being away from logged areas for more than short periods of time.

The trails initially were well-maintained and well-blazed with many PCT markers. This ended abruptly when I left Shasta-Trinity National Forest for Klamath National Forest. Immediately all the blazes and markers ended and I promptly took the wrong trail, though only for a few yards as I quickly realised it was heading the wrong way.

For one day I was in the Salmon Trinity Alps Primitive Area (designated the Trinity Alps Wilderness in 1984), enjoyable wild country with rugged rocky ridges and beautiful lakes, then it was back into Klamath National Forest with its continuing lack of signs and plenty of side trails where

The mountains of Northern California with Mount Shasta in the distance

I could go wrong so I had to concentrate on the route. Although the mountains here were much lower than those in the High Sierra, apart from the stratovolcanoes, with summits in the 7,000-9,000 feet range, timberline was also much lower at around 6,000 feet (due to being at a higher latitude) so the rise above the forests was about the same. The PCT was often at or above timberline between Castella and Seiad Valley so there were more views and less forest walking than in the lower section before Castella. The timberline trees here were often western white pines and I noticed that they had downward curved snow-shedding branches like the red firs, something they'd lacked in the High Sierra where they grew lower down.

As I traversed on a good trail above the South Russian River I had my third bear sighting, this one quite a small animal that ran off crashing through the undergrowth as soon as it saw me. This area wasn't a designated wilderness when I was there but just two years later it became the

Russian Wilderness to protect the granite peaks, glaciated valleys, lovely lakes and magnificent forests. I had a camp by Paynes Lake, set in a beautiful glacial cirque with a steep rocky peak at its head and big red firs and mountain hemlocks on its shores. Other hikers were leaving as I arrived, one of them with a pack donkey. No-one else arrived and I had one of the most beautiful campsites for many weeks to myself.

Mount Shasta came into view again as I approached the Marble Mountain Wilderness. It didn't seem to be getting any further away. The landscape became more rugged and dramatic as I entered the Marble Mountains, especially on a traverse around Kidder Valley. There was much rock, snow and meltwater along with many nice little mountain pools. I was even more impressed on my second day in the Marble Mountains starting my journal entry with 'A splendid day! Best mountain scenery since the High Sierra'. Timberline trails, lovely high mountain pools, marble pavements with above the rocky peaks of Black Mountain and Marble Mountain itself – this was wonderful hiking country. Some of the peaks, notably Black Mountain, were built of pale limestone with dark caps of metamorphic rock and reminded me slightly of the hills Penyghent and Ingleborough in the limestone country of the Yorkshire Dales in the Pennine hills of England.

Other hikers warned me that bears sometimes raided camp sites here so as there was plenty of bear dung on the trail I hung my food at my one camp in the Marble Mountain Wilderness. Although I had no views from this camp below Buckhorn Mountain the fine trees made up for it as did the bird life. Two kestrels flew overhead as I approached the site and

The trail enters the Salmon Trinity Alps Primitive Area

once camp was made I watched three red-breasted nuthatches flitting about in the branches above my tent. High above a red-tailed hawk circled then a tiny rufous humming bird flew into camp and whirred in front of a flower before buzzing away.

One more day of hiking and I arrived in Seiad Valley beside the Klamath River. The last seven miles were a hot and tiring road walk, necessary because of the need to use the highway bridge across the river and because the land alongside the river is private and there's no access for hikers. The town was another tiny one set in a steep-sided canyon but as elsewhere it had the necessary facilities for hikers – post office, café, store, laundromat and shower. I was surprised (and pleased) to meet Larry here as I'd guessed he would be far ahead by now. He had taken two fewer days than me to get here but was then held up because the post was delayed and he needed his supply parcel as it contained new boots. Apparently this delay was due to a chemical spill on Interstate 5. We pondered how events outside the wilds and seemingly irrelevant to the PCT can still have an effect. In Seiad Valley I also learnt that the smoke I could see to the west was from a big forest fire covering 2000 acres. I hoped it wouldn't advance near the trail.

In my mail were the maps for Oregon. Soon I would be leaving California, having walked some 1500 miles through the State. Mike had sent more copies of the North Lake Tahoe Bonanza which I mailed to Warren and to friends and family back home and also to Delree, the woman who'd given us a lift into Los Angeles from Acton to buy gear for the High Sierra, as I had a letter from her with a new address – she'd left Acton and moved into L.A. I gave a copy of the newspaper article to the store owner too, who put it up on the wall. Also in my mail was a new pair of shorts – 'just in time!' I wrote in my journal. The old ones were becoming rather risqué.

Larry's new boots finally arrived the next day and we left Seiad Valley together for the usual steep hot dry climb, this one for 3700 feet to Lookout Spring where we found a trail crew at work. The leader, Bill, had built the stone trough and put in the pipe for the spring four years earlier and was now clearing it out and putting up a sign. He and his partner were out for 10 days on the PCT doing trail work with four horses for themselves and their supplies. We were grateful for their work and especially the spring, whose water we drank copiously. Setting out in the middle of the day, necessary due to waiting for Larry's boots, was not a good idea. Early morning would have been far cooler for this steep climb.

Leaving the trail crew at their work and with full water containers we went on a short distance to the Lower Devils Peak Lookout, which lay at the end of a narrow rocky ridge. The old disused lookout was just a roofless shell set on a small flat area above steep drops. The place made for a fine campsite with wide-ranging views. A red sunset and a bright half-moon lit the sky and I was looking forward to sleeping out in such a splendid spot. Mosquitoes defeated this idea however and, as I had for many nights now, I pitched the tent to fend them off.

Larry left an hour before me the next morning. I never saw him again. Hiking together had worked well and we'd become friends without ever being really close. I realised that I didn't actually know that much about him. We'd not discussed our home lives much or our views on matters outside hiking and the wilderness. Mostly we didn't talk at all beyond practical matters to do with the days hike and camp site. He'd been part of my life for most of three months however and suddenly he vanished from it.

With my new tree guide I was able to identify two new ones the next day – graceful Brewers Spruce and sparse Knobcone Pine. I was still enjoying the wide range of trees in the forests, something that was to be one of my main memories of the PCT. The day was again hot and there was no water on the trail except for a couple of springs. I camped by the second one at Alex Hole. The guidebook said the next water sources were 15 and 25 miles away so I'd need to carry full bottles from here. I was now heading back east to the Cascades at the end of the PCT's loop into the Klamath Mountains.

'A lazy day. That is, I felt slow but still did 16 miles' is the start of my entry for the next day. Somewhere on a heavily logged slope I crossed into Oregon, saying farewell to California after 1550 miles and four months. The border was unmarked and the location uninspiring. Today there's a PCT sign and a hiker registration box. Overall it was a day of pleasant hill crest walking with many views – Mount Shasta still and my first glimpse of Mount McLoughlin, the first volcano in Oregon.

Along the trail I found several notes giving route advice addressed to Susie, who I'd last seen two weeks before, from one Jay J.Johnson, who I'd heard about from other hikers. He was on an amazing journey. Nearly nine months previously he'd set off to walk south on the 2,000 mile Appalachian Trail in the Eastern USA, then row through the Everglades, cycle across Texas and start back north on the PCT. I wondered if I'd meet him and hear about this epic journey. The notes were untouched but old-looking, which suggested Susie was some way behind me and even more behind Jay.

Apart from the notes several kestrels, one harrying a soaring red-tailed hawk, a couple of deer and some crashing, whirring blue grouse were all that added interest to the walking until I reached Wrangle Gap Camp, described in the guidebook as 'the answer to an exhausted hiker's prayer. This little-used recreation site .... has a large stone shelter complete with fireplace, 2 stoves, tables and even a sink with running water!' Given this description I was a little surprised when I arrived to discover ranks of white tents and a shelter full of trestle tables and cooking gear. Even more startling were the lines of people sitting at desks writing away furiously! A bizarre sight in this forest setting, looking as it did like a displaced examination room. Which, in fact, was what it was for the writers were students on a geology course finishing their final reports. Being outnumbered I camped some distance away in the woods and managed to do without the sink and its running water. Later in the evening I chatted to the friendly students who were from the Southern Oregon University in Ashland.

CHAPTER 4

FORESTS, LAKES & VOLCANOES: OREGON

WRANGLE GAP TO THE COLUMBIA RIVER
August 1 to August 26
444 miles

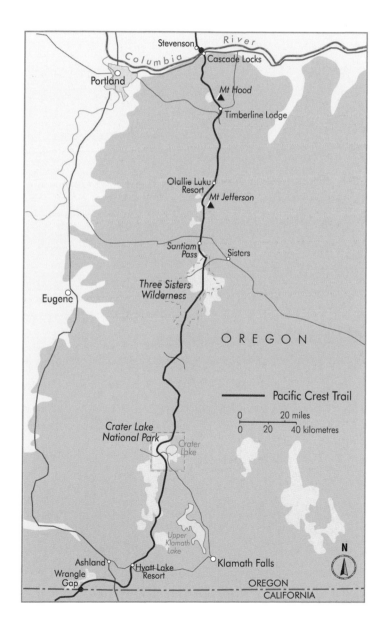

Stevenson
Columbia River
Cascade Locks
Portland
Mt Hood
Timberline Lodge
Olallie Lake Resort
Mt Jefferson
Santiam Pass
Sisters
Three Sisters Wilderness
Eugene
OREGON
Pacific Crest Trail
0   20 miles
0   20   40 kilometres
Crater Lake National Park
Crater Lake
Upper Klamath Lake
Ashland
Wrangle Gap
Hyatt Lake Resort
Klamath Falls
N
OREGON
CALIFORNIA

125

The walk through Oregon began with an urban break in the city of Ashland. My first full day in the State I walked just four miles along a dirt road before a car carrying some of the geology students stopped and offered me a lift. Their two weeks sojourn in the woods was over and they were returning to Ashland. I'd been considering hitch-hiking there anyway in order to sort out my broken pack so this ride was welcome. I was in the big city by lunchtime (not that big I guess but with a population of 20,000+ it seemed huge to me). As it was Sunday the only outdoor store I could find was closed so I decided to stay overnight, which actually became two nights. Ashland is famous for the Oregon Shakespeare Festival, which was on at the time so the town was very much Shakespeare themed. I thought of seeing a play but the one on that night was *Henry V*, which didn't appeal. I think *A Midsummer Night's Dream* would have been more appropriate for my walk. Instead of a play I went to a party – beer, music and talking. This was the students' end of course party to which I'd been invited and was just like the many student parties I'd been to back home when I was at college. I was also offered a floor to sleep on, which was welcome.

Much of my second day in Ashland was spent in the Sun Cycle outdoor shop deliberating about a new pack. As I'd suspected mine couldn't be repaired, at least not here. Ideally I wanted another one with an internal frame – one as similar as possible to mine in fact. However none of the internal frame models in the store were anything like as big as my 100 litre monster. I did try, dumping the contents of my old pack on the floor and attempting to stuff them into the biggest internal frame pack they had, much to the amusement of the tolerant and helpful staff. It was quickly evident that there was no way it would all fit. This meant I had to overcome my prejudices and consider an external frame pack (prejudices formed by using one on the Pennine Way in England six years earlier and not liking it), which meant one with a separate rigid tubular frame from which the pack hung. I ended up with a pack from The North Face with what I hoped was a promising name, Back Magic 1, chosen mainly because it was big enough but also because this was the model Dave had been given back in Mammoth Lakes and he'd been very pleased with it. With more pockets and compartments and the external frame it was as different as possible from my pack so I'd have to relearn how to pack it and how to adjust the straps for a comfortable carry, both of which were now automatic with my old one. I was reluctant to part with it but I didn't want to hike another 1000 miles with an uncomfortable pack. The new one claimed to have a capacity of 87 litres but was at least as roomy as the old one (testing packs over the last 30 years has since taught me that litres are not a fixed quantity when it comes to pack volume!). The pack that had accompanied me this far, an old friend now, I sadly sent off to its British makers for repair. I hoped I would grow fond of the new one quickly, especially as it cost me $177.50 I didn't really have.

Both the packs I used on the PCT would seem like heavyweight monsters to today's thru-hikers. Back then lightweight packs made from materials like Dyneema and cuben fibre didn't exist. Other gear was heavier and bulkier too so large capacity packs that could handle big heavy loads were needed. Despite the ruggedness failures were common as the suspension systems were complex with many components. Larry, Dave and Scott all changed packs during the hike.

After this city interlude I was glad to return to the trail and the woods. Two of the students gave me a lift up to Siskiyou Gap, where they'd picked me up. Now I could really start hiking the PCT through Oregon. Much of the trail in Oregon is fairly level and it has the reputation for being the easiest walking on the PCT, though there are some long dry sections where water has to be carried, making for a heavier load. In Southern Oregon the PCT follows the crest of the Cascades as here they are low, forested hills with occasional rock outcrops. I made only eight miles this first day though, stopping at the large Grouse Gap Shelter, which I shared with two families here on their annual outing. They arrived with a six week old kitten called Caesar, which they left with me while they went for a walk up Mount Ashland, which made for an unusual and entertaining few hours as I played with the kitten and ensured it didn't wander off. On their return I was invited to join in their hot dog and toasted marshmallow supper as a big moon rose through the clouds above the still visible Mount Shasta, giving a dramatic night sky.

The first week on the PCT in Oregon wasn't the most memorable part of the walk. The trail meandered through forests without much ascent or descent and without many views. This was multiple-use forest and there was much clear-cutting which gave an unnatural patchwork look to the forest with contrasting squares of regenerating forest, cleared forest and mature forest. On the first day from Grouse Gap the dramatic volcanic rock tower called Pilot Knob dominated the landscape. Further away I could see Mount Shasta dipping in and out of drifting clouds and again there were glimpses of Mount McLoughlin. This was my first full day with the new pack and after 20 miles I decided I liked it though the rattle of the split-rings that attached the pack to the frame was a little irritating.

There was much wildlife in the forest though – deer, squirrels, kestrels, grouse, ravens, hawks, humming birds – and where untouched the trees were marvellous. I identified two more – grand fir and noble fir – and reckoned the tiny booklet called *Pacific Coast Tree Finder* one of my best purchases. Twenty-eight years later I was to take the exact same booklet on the Pacific Northwest Trail and find it just as useful. From it I'd already identified nine pines, six firs, four cedars, two spruces, two hemlocks and Douglas fir, which isn't actually a true fir at all. The richness of the forest continued to astound me.

Dotted through the forest in Southern Oregon are many large lakes, some with an attendant fishing resort prepared to hold parcels and mail for PCT hikers. Two days into Oregon I reached the first of these, Hyatt Lake Resort. There was a good café but the store was the poorest I'd yet seen for hiking food. With anglers as its main market all it sold was beer, soft drinks, crisps and candy bars. I had evening meals in my supply box but not much else so for breakfasts and day snacks I bought fifteen candy bars, which I reckoned should get me to the next resort in a couple of days and, hopefully, a better store for hikers. I did eat dinner and breakfast in the Hyatt Lake café, which saved me some food for later on.

Lake of the Woods Resort, reached two days later, did have a slightly better store, in that it had cheese, sugar and trail mix as well as candy bars, plus a good café where I had a lunch that was far better than a handful of those bars. On my shopping list I ticked off three items out of ten. At Hyatt Lake I'd ticked just one.

That evening it rained slightly for the first time in a few weeks and there was a cool breeze off Fourmile Lake by which I was camped. I noticed that it was already dark at 9 p.m. It was closer now to the autumn equinox than the summer solstice.

North of Fourmile Lake (actually a reservoir) the country was wilder and unspoilt. It's now protected in the Sky Lakes Wilderness. The PCT ran right through this wilderness-to-be but didn't visit any of the lakes. I soon passed Mount McLoughlin as the landscape grew more mountainous. The dominant peak was still Mount Shasta though, now far away to the south. Ahead I could see the jagged peaks around Crater Lake and beyond them the spire of Mount Thielsen. In places there were still a few snow patches to cross. I had one camp in the future Sky Lakes Wilderness beside Honeymoon Creek. In the evening rain began to fall and I could hear long slow rolls of thunder in the distance. Suddenly the storm reached me and from all around came echoing, rolling thunder and flashes of lightning. I was glad to be in the woods and not on an exposed site on a mountainside. The storm passed on as quickly as it arrived leaving a clear starry sky though I heard distant rumbles of thunder for hours afterwards.

A mostly viewless day in thick mountain hemlock forest led to roadside Mazama Campground and Crater Lake National Park, the only national park in Oregon. Just once, on a traverse called Watershed Divide, was there a view of the rock fang called Union Peak and the peaks ringing the south end of Crater Lake. I needed a permit to hike and camp in the backcountry in the park but these were self-issuing and there was a box of them where the PCT entered the park (today all thru-hikers need to do is sign the register at the same spot).

Mazama Campground offered an outdoor slide lecture on the Cascade volcanoes which I found useful and informative. A knowledge of geology always adds to the appreciation of a landscape and this volcanic area was one I didn't know much about. Wanting to learn more the next day I bought a copy of Stephen Harris's *Fire and Ice: The Story of the Cascade Volcanoes* (the updated current version is called *Fire Mountains of the West)*. From this excellent book, which I carried for the rest of the walk, I learnt that Crater Lake is not really in a crater but in a caldera, which is the hole left when a volcano blows its top and then collapses in on itself.

At the time of my walk the PCT didn't actually visit Crater Lake itself but stayed in the forest out of sight of the lake. I couldn't imagine though that any hikers didn't walk the short distance to the lake. It's the most impressive sight on the PCT in Southern Oregon. Today the PCT has been divided into two here – equestrians are still directed down the old forested trail, hikers up to Crater Lake.

At the Crater Lake post office I collected a big food box – it was around nine days to the next supply point – and then topped up my supplies at the grocery store, which was far better than those at the fishing resorts. I noticed that my estimated date of collection was July 28th. Today was August 10th. The High Sierra was the reason of course. At Weldon I'd been two days behind schedule. By Echo Lakes this had risen to twelve days. I hadn't yet made up any time. In the PCT Register there were no entries from Larry or Susie and both had mail waiting for them here. I couldn't imagine Larry was behind me but did wonder if he'd stuck to the PCT and not come here.

Supplies sorted I walked on to magnificent Crater Lake, one of the great sights of the PCT. Despite having seen many pictures it was still breath-taking. With a depth of 1,932 feet it's the deepest lake in the USA and the seventh deepest in the world. The basin it lies in is nearly 4,000 feet deep and the lake is five to six miles across. In geological terms it's a very new lake, formed around 7,000 years ago when a 12,000 foot volcano, now named Mazama, erupted and disintegrated leaving behind a caldera that slowly filled with rain and snow to become Crater Lake. When Mazama erupted an estimated 12 cubic miles of volcanic material was blasted into the sky, traces of which have been found as far afield as British Columbia and Alberta, far to the north in Canada. The water in Crater Lake is very pure as there are few sediments and very little surface water runs into it. None runs out. This purity accounts for the brilliant ultramarine colour that greets you as you reach the rim and gaze 900 feet down to this fairy tale lake. Rarely have I been so moved on seeing a view as on first seeing Crater Lake and I spent hours walking along the rim and staring across it, fascinated by the circular shape, the deep blue colour, the volcanic cone of Wizard Island rising out of the water, and the coloured rock strata of the unbroken cliffs stretching in a great curve round it.

At Crater Lake I also had my first sighting of a bald eagle, one of the birds I most wanted to see on the walk. These magnificent white-headed eagles were once endangered but have made a good recovery due to conservation measures. PCT hikers today are far more likely to see bald eagles than in 1982. Slightly smaller than the golden eagle, which I was familiar with from the Scottish Highlands, bald eagles are fish eaters that frequent large bodies of water. Whilst I saw other large raptors that may have been bald or golden eagles they were usually too far away for certain identification. It was not until I reached Lake Chelan near the end of the walk that I was to see another bald eagle. I love seeing eagles, both because they are impressive in themselves but also because they signify wilderness. I did have a tiny pair of 8x20 binoculars with me that helped with bird and animal watching and identification and I watched the bald eagle soaring over Crater Lake through these.

Unsurprisingly Crater Lake is popular and this being the height of the summer season there were many other people around. Access is easy too as a road runs right round the rim. Eventually I tore myself away from the lake and dropped back down into the forest to camp. I don't know if this was legal or not. Today wild camping is allowed in the park's backcountry as long as you're

Wizard Island and Crater Lake
Crater Lake

a mile from a road – the PCTA publishes a map showing the areas this includes. That night it rained heavily and I woke to thick clouds and a cold, wet wind. Unable to resist another look I returned to Crater Lake the next day. With sunshine gone the scene was very different. Grey threads of cloud raced over the rough dull water and round the tops of the volcanic cones of the islands, mist wreaths that gave an other-worldly air to the scene.

I couldn't stay long though as the next water lay 25 miles away across the strange Oregon Desert. This is a flat area of sand made of pumice and ash from the Mazama eruption through which all water drains and which is dotted with widely spaced, stunted lodgepole pines whose roots just stretch down far enough to reach the streams that run underground below the pumice. I was hoping there might be some snow patches left but I couldn't rely on this. Ironically, it was raining heavily when I left Crater Lake for this long waterless section.

The walking was easy though and the 25 miles were soon done. Sometimes I forgot just how fit I now was. The trail took me over the Oregon Desert then around Mount Thielsen, a 9178 foot high volcanic remnant that forms a splendid jagged spire of twisted yellow and red rock strata. Being the central plug of a volcano, the rest of the mountain having been eroded away, Mount Thielsen is the geological opposite of Crater Lake and also the visual opposite – a soaring rock pinnacle rather than water-filled deep hole. Volcanoes like this in the Cascades are known as Matterhorn Peaks because of their steep pointed shape. I had a superb view of this fine peak from my camp beside Mount Thielsen Creek on a well-used site. Mount Thielsen looked particularly impressive at dawn when the rock shone in the rising sun. In my journal I wrote 'best camp site and view I've had since the Marble Mountains'. The night was frosty for the first time in weeks and in the morning the snow patches on the trail were rock hard and there was ice on puddles. Not long after leaving I met a party of twelve heavily laden boy scouts toiling up to the Mount Thielsen Creek camp site. I was glad they hadn't arrived the night before. It wasn't a large site and I'd enjoyed the quiet and the solitude.

Later in the day I met a PCT hiker heading south. He was just doing the Oregon section of the trail. 'The mosquitoes have been terrible' he warned me and sure enough they promptly increased in number as I headed for the interestingly named Nip and Tuck Lakes where I camped. These forest lakes lay on the old Oregon Skyline Trail, which ran end-to-end through the State. It was built in the 1930s but was superseded by the PCT which often takes a different route. I planned on following the old trail here though because it had water sources, unlike the PCT, and was nine miles shorter. An extra nine miles of forest walking didn't seem to have any advantages. During the day I crossed into the Williamette National Forest. On the boundary there was a PCT sign reading 195 miles to California and 219 to Washington. I was almost halfway through Oregon.

A long hot forested mosquito-ridden walk led to Cascade Summit on Odell Lake, my next supply point (nearby Shelter Cove Resort is used by today's hikers). I barely stopped all day due to the bugs and arrived sweaty, thirsty and tired. The post office was a cupboard in the small store and only open in the summer for PCT hikers and long-stay visitors. In the register I discovered that Larry was five days ahead of me and Scott and Dave nine. The store had the best selection of trail food and hiking accessories I'd seen in anywhere this small so I was able to supplement my dried meals with some good trail mix and granola bars and buy stove fuel, candles, insect repellent and a pot scrub. Just garlic powder, packet soup and socks remained on my shopping list. There was also a café so I'd no need to eat dried food here. Camping and showers were free for PCT hikers too, a very welcome touch. In fact Cascade Summit was a great spot. I was joined here by a southbound hiker called Mark who was just doing the Oregon and Washington PCT (I say 'just', it's a thousand miles!) so I had company in camp for the first time in a couple of weeks.

Mid-August turned out to be Boy Scout season in Oregon as I encountered literally hundreds of them during the next few days including a mass camp at Middle Rosary Lake that filled the woods for hundreds of yards. I passed this by, as I did Wait Here Lake, after hesitating a little, tempted by the name, and finally camped by Bobby Lake. I was still in fairly flat forest but was approaching the Three Sisters Wilderness, the first of a series of wilderness areas the PCT runs through in the northern half of Oregon.

I still had a mostly viewless day in the pond-dotted forest though, but there was one brilliant experience that made the day stand out. Hurrying along towards the peaks that I occasionally glimpsed tantalisingly through the trees, I caught a movement in a small, shallow, lily-dotted pond beside the trail. I stopped and looked and soon saw an otter and three cubs in the water. Slowly and quietly I took off my pack and sat down on it. I then spent half an hour watching the otters swimming and diving in the clear water. They glanced at me occasionally but seemed curious and wary rather than afraid. Often they dived closely in a group, arching their backs together in the air. When they came nearer – just a few feet away – I could see them swimming underwater. They made loud hissing noises and occasionally high-pitched squeaks as they swam. Once, they came out of the water to lie draped over a small rock in the middle of the pond and as I was leaving they all climbed onto a log. Watching the otters was a wonderful experience that took me completely out of myself. It was one of the wildlife highlights of the walk. The following day I saw two more of these beautiful creatures swimming together in Island Lake.

The Three Sisters Wilderness is unusual because here a whole collection of volcanoes are grouped together whereas elsewhere in Oregon they are well spread out with often dozens of miles between them. It's a popular backpacking area and as I reached it I began to meet other hikers, fourteen in total that first day. Three of these had seen Larry who'd gained another day on me and Scott and Dave who were a day ahead of Larry. Maybe, I thought, I might catch up with Scott and Dave.

Finally leaving the confines of the forest the trail climbed up and around Koosah Mountain from where I could see Diamond Peak not far away and, looking back, the already distant spire of Mount Thielsen. Then came a really special view of glorious rocky mountains – symmetrical Bachelor Butte, ragged Broken Top and red rock capped South Sister with beyond it Middle Sister and North Sister. I wanted to camp with a view of these mountains but the shores of Camelot Lake were already lined with the tents of others with the same intention so I went on to slightly

Broken Top rising above the forest

less crowded though still scenic Sisters Mirror Lake. Here I had a surprise. I heard someone approaching and looked up to see Wayne Fuiten, whom I hadn't seen since Weldon, three months ago. Wayne wasn't surprised to see me though as he'd been following my entries in the trail registers since Crater Lake. His walk had been a complicated one.

He'd taken two weeks off to allow some of the snow to melt and had then walked south from Northern California to Weldon before hitch-hiking north again and continuing towards Canada. I was now to see him most days during my remaining time in Oregon though as before his regulated walking style and my haphazard one didn't gel so we didn't walk together often. We tended to use the same camp sites however as these were far and few between. That first evening we spent hours talking about our adventures and the places we'd seen.

I woke to a mist on the lake and dew on the grass. Gray jays were flitting round the camp. It was the start of one of the most memorable days of the walk. In my journal that evening I wrote 'A superb day! One of the best! Glorious mountain country and fantastic volcanic features. Hiked through meadows, forests and parkland past the Three Sisters; South Sister large rounded and complex, Middle Sister a pure cone and North Sister a jagged rock remnant. Plus glaciers on all of them. And then lava flows, curling rivers of frozen basalt and huge mounds of pyroclastic cinders and a switch-backing path up the flow into the breached wall of Collier Cone'. Ahead further volcanic peaks soared above the dark forest. In a line fading away to the north were Mount Washington, Three-Fingered Jacket, Mount Jefferson and, barely visible, Mount Hood, beyond which lay the Columbia River and Washington State. As well as the big mountains –

Clockwise: The trail approaching North Sister
The trail winding up the lava flows of Collier Cone
Collier Cone

the Three Sisters are all over 10,000 feet high – I really liked the sparse almost parkland like tree-scattered volcanic uplands such as Wickiup Plain and the minor volcanic peaks – Broken Top, The Wife, The Husband and Little Brother. In fact there was nothing about this landscape that displeased me. It was all a delight. On the trails I'd seen more hikers than on just about any other day of the walk and that night I camped by another scenic lake, South Mathieu, along with Wayne and a few other people.

This was the start of a succession of fine landscapes that stretched all the way to Canada. Although there would still be days deep in the trees and areas of logged, despoiled forest to cross these would be mere brief interruptions between wilderness areas. Since Echo Lake the PCT had been more low-key and gentle, with rather too many roads and logged areas in the quiet forests. That 850 mile section through Northern California and Southern Oregon, which

Rest stop on an Oregon lava flow with Mount Washington in the background
Mount Washington, Three-Fingered Jack and Mount Jefferson

had taken me 53 days, is the part of the PCT I'd suggest skipping for any hiker without time to do the whole trail. There were high points, especially the Marble Mountains and Crater Lake, but overall the wilderness feel, the beauty of the landscape, and the sense of adventure didn't compare with the areas to the north and south. I didn't realise this that first day in the Three Sisters Wilderness of course. I was just pleased to be in such grand country. It was only as the weeks went by that I realised the walk had changed and that the wilder and more exciting mountains were back to being the norm rather the exception.

From South Mathieu Lake there was much walking on rough, brittle, cinder-like basalt lava flows as I crossed a highway at McKenzie Pass and then entered the Mount Washington Wilderness. Mount Washington is another volcanic plug Matterhorn peak, with a fine soaring spire. A long haul up the dark unstable lava of the almost barren Belknap Crater, which was like walking on a slag heap, was a tough test of my lightweight shoes and the balance of my new pack. Both, I was pleased to find out, were fine on this rugged terrain. The landscape looked like that of an inhospitable alien planet in a science-fiction film. All was brown and black twisted rock. There were barely any plants. It was easy to imagine the lava molten and flowing sinuously down the mountainside. The walking was hot and sweaty as there was no shade from the sun and the dark rocks soon became hot to the touch. From the col with Little Belknap I could see back to the Three Sisters and ahead to Mounts Washington and Jefferson. I was becoming used to seeing these high peaks rising above the forest in almost a straight line. Round them rolled undulating forested green hills. There were closer views of Mount Washington as the trail traversed its flanks before the day ended with a descent into a ghostly burned lodgepole pine forest, the stark dead trees pointing forlornly at the sky, that led to Santiam Pass, where a highway crosses the mountains, and Santiam Lodge, a combined Presbyterian Retreat and Youth Camp and American Youth Hostel, the only such one on the PCT (and now long closed). Here I stayed with Joe, a southbound PCT hiker who was hoping to at least reach the High Sierra before the first autumn snows started to block the trail. The lodge was a good place for a shower and dinner and relaxation, though I commented in my journal: 'slept on a typical Y.H. creaky bed'. I had a supply

box here along with mail that included a note from Warren asking when I thought I'd be in Stevenson, my first supply point in Washington State, as he wanted to send me a special item. I was intrigued!

The next morning Wayne turned up with his family from Seattle, where he'd been having a short break, and offered me a lift to the nearby town of Sisters where I could add to my supplies, there being no store at Santiam Lodge. As we were leaving Mark, the PCT hiker I'd camped with at Cascade Summit a week before, turned up very thirsty and tired. He'd been without water for some time and had hoped to make it here the night before but had ended up having a waterless camp in the lava fields. The trip into Sisters was a quick one and I was back on the trail before midday, soon rounding the rocky spires of Three-Fingered

Wayne Fuiten on the trail below Three-Fingered Jack

Jack, another Matterhorn peak. I was especially impressed with the convoluted red strata of the north side of this ragged triple-spired mountain.Late in the day the skies clouded over as I entered the Mount Jefferson Wilderness – the wilderness areas were coming thick and fast now. I'd just pitched the tent beside Rockville Lake when Wayne turned up. Rain soon began to fall and there many loud rumbles of thunder and a gusty wind. The latter didn't deter the mosquitoes though and I was soon driven into the tent where I lay reading and writing by candlelight. The mosquitoes had been pretty bad for a few weeks now. 'When will they stop?' I wrote in my journal.

More rain and thunder woke me during the night but by dawn it was calm and the sun soon dried the tent. I left early, heading for Mount Jefferson, whose graceful cone had been slowly becoming more dominant in the view for several days. The Mount Jefferson Wilderness is popular and I met quite a few other hikers. I soon saw why as the mountain and the landscape round it is beautiful. I found it one of the most attractive areas on the whole walk and 10, 497 foot Mount Jefferson one of the finest peaks. That evening I again wrote 'a superb day!' in my journal. The whole day I had excellent views of Mount Jefferson and its glaciers. The guidebook warned that creek crossings could be problematic here but this late in the season they were shallow, the most notorious, fast flowing Russell Creek, no more than ankle deep. Milk Creek was true to its name, being chalky white with sediment washed down from the glaciers. I decided not to drink out of that one. The heart of the area was Jefferson Park, a lovely timberline area of meadows and tree groves on the edge of which I camped by Russell Lake with a view across the parkland to the great glacier-smeared north-west face of the mountain. This memorable day ended with a wonderful calm evening with subtle shades of pink and blue as the sun set on the snowfields across the lake. It was almost perfect. But not quite for, as I wrote in my journal, 'the mosquitoes have been bad all day'. I was prepared to put up with them for such beauty though and I was really enjoying being at timberline again.

As with all the mountain and timberline sections of the trail in wooded Oregon I soon left the Mount Jefferson Wilderness behind for a descent into the forest. Green would be the colour for the PCT in Oregon, it spends so much time in the trees. First though I climbed over late-lingering snow patches to a ridge that gave excellent views back to Jefferson Park and Mount Jefferson. Then there was a long descent over glacial rubble and more snow that took me out of the open country (and the Wilderness Area) and back into the forest. Down in the trees I headed for Olallie Lake where there was a resort that provided a lunch of Coca-Cola and donuts and enough candy bars and trail mix for the next few days (today the resort carries 'hiker foods and supplies'). The lake was tranquil with a good view of Mount Jefferson.

Mount Jefferson

After more forest walking I again camped with Wayne, at a quiet spot called Trooper Springs.

A forested day with just one brief view of Mount Hood followed, a day of easy walking on flat terrain mostly in the Warm Springs Indian Reservation. Away from the more scenic landscapes there were few other hikers. I thought this might mean there would be more wildlife but I only saw one deer. During the day I crossed the 45th Meridian – half way between the Equator and the North Pole. That evening Wayne arrived again as I was setting up camp by Timothy Lake, the last water for quite a while. Preparing to boil water I lit my stove only to see flames licking round the filler cap on the fuel tank. I turned the stove off and managed to smother the fire before the cap blew off, as it was designed to do to prevent the whole fuel tank exploding if the pressure grew too great. Cooking with gasoline can be exciting! I'd always been careful to point the cap away from my tent so that if it did ignite the inevitable jet of flame wouldn't burn it down. Once the stove had cooled I replaced the cap with the new one I had bought back in Mount Shasta. I hoped this would last until the end of the walk as I probably couldn't get another.

I was now heading for Mount Hood, the last of the Oregon volcanoes and also the highest at 11,235 feet, and Timberline Lodge, which lay on its flanks. The day began in particularly fine

Timothy Lake

forest above the Salmon River with stands of big majestic Douglas fir, western hemlock, western red cedar, Alaska cedar and more. I never tired of these huge magnificent trees, even after hundreds of miles of forest walking. Mount Hood appeared in glimpses through them. Then came an 1800 foot climb up to Timberline Lodge during which the full glory of Mount Hood was revealed.

A curious and slightly disturbing incident occurred during this climb. As I ascended one particularly steep section I could see a hiker sitting on the ground where it eased off. As I reached him he pulled aside his jacket to reveal a pistol in a holster and started talking about how he was ready to shoot anybody who messed with him. He said this while staring into space, almost as if I wasn't there. As soon as I got my breath back I said farewell and walked on as quickly as I could. When I looked back he was still sitting there. Much further on in the walk another incident occurred that made me think of him but that comes later.

Timberline Lodge is a very grand stone and timber building and the centre of the Timberline Lodge Ski Resort that provides year round skiing on Mount Hood's permanent snowfields. It was a government project, built in the 1930s by unemployed craftspeople during the Depression, and is now a designated National Historic Landmark. I had a

The Barlow Road crosses the southern slopes of Mount Hood

food parcel here at the store, which was basically a gift shop without any provisions suitable for hikers, and ate a huge and tasty if expensive meal in the restaurant before having a few beers with Wayne, who turned up shortly after me and was more interested in the bar than in food. We then walked off a few hundred yards to sleep under the trees. Next morning I returned to the Lodge for a hearty breakfast before setting off on another superb timberline day across Mount Hood. For ten or so miles the PCT coincided with the Timberline Trail that goes right round the mountain. The walking was fairly arduous as the trail climbed in and out of many glacial creek canyons but this was easily ignored as the detailed views of the alpine landscape of Mount Hood, replete with icefalls, cliffs, glaciers and hanging valleys, was marvellous. Mount Hood is certainly a beautiful mountain, competing with Mount Jefferson for the most attractive in Oregon in my mind. Hood was more rugged, Jefferson more graceful. I couldn't choose between them. I really appreciated the trail here though as for once in Oregon it was actually on the mountain itself rather than below it. Skiers were out early on some of the runs near the Lodge as avalanche danger in summer meant they closed at lunchtime. There were many hikers too.

Beyond Mount Hood I could see ahead to big bulky Mount Adams, the first Washington State volcano, and back to Mount Jefferson and the Three Sisters. Eventually the mountain was left

Mount Hood

for the forest and I descended out of the Mount Hood Wilderness to camp in an old logged area at Lolo Pass where I was soon joined by Wayne. Although in the trees there was still a view of Mount Hood towering above us but I was soon driven into the tent by the mosquitos which I could then hear humming outside the insect net door. Earlier the little biting flies that had been an occasional nuisance for the last few weeks were overactive, buzzing round me and repeatedly trying to remove chunks of flesh. There were high cirrus clouds and I wondered if a storm front was coming in and rising humidity was making the flies more active.

Like virtually all PCT hikers then and now I was planning on leaving the PCT the next day for the far more scenic Eagle Creek Trail. This isn't part of the PCT because it's impassable for horses but, like Crater Lake, it's not to be missed by hikers. The 'official' PCT is a gentle descent through the forest, the Eagle Creek Trail is an exciting descent down a cliff-rimmed canyon. Various volcanoes bobbed briefly in and out of view on the initial walk in the forest. Then came a stony traverse in open terrain around Indian Mountain from which I was excited to catch my first views of Mount Rainier, far away still, and Mount St. Helens from which rose a steam plume, an aftermath of the big eruption that had taken place just two years before.

I left Indian Mountain on a very steep, jarring descent down the rough unmaintained Indian Springs Trail that led to a junction with the Eagle Creek Trail. Down this trail I went, a pleasant wooded path at first but its character changed dramatically on reaching Eagle Creek itself. Here the trail began a long traverse down the steep-sided canyon past beautiful waterfalls and deep pools. The centrepiece of this magnificent ravine is Tunnel Falls, where the East Fork of Eagle Creek drops 150 feet into the main creek. Here the narrow, exhilarating trail is blasted into the side of the vertical cliff some 75 feet above the river before passing behind the waterfall in a spray-drenched rock passageway – a superb and imaginative piece of trail building. I could have wandered up and down here for many hours. Wayne and I had arranged to meet here in the

Wayne Fuiten and Tunnel Falls

late afternoon as that's the only time the sun shines on Tunnel Falls and we spent some time photographing each other on the narrow trail.

Unsurprisingly the Eagle Creek Trail is very popular and camping is restricted to certain spots. Beyond Tunnel Falls we descended to Blue Ridge Camp, which at 1120 feet was the lowest on the walk so far, and slept out under the trees. For once there were no mosquitoes.

Eagle Creek is one of the many creeks that pour down from the mountains either side into the huge Columbia River, which splits the Cascades here. Rising far to the north in the Rocky Mountains in Canada this 1,243 mile long river is the largest in the Pacific Northwest region. Between Oregon and Washington State the river runs through the Columbia River Gorge for

80 miles. In places this massive gorge is 4,000 feet deep. Waterfalls pour down the sides and it is these that gave their name to the Cascades, which were known as 'the mountains by the cascades' by the first western explorers. This was soon shortened to just 'the cascades' and the name became applied to the whole range that extends many hundreds of miles either side of the Columbia River Gorge. The actual name 'Cascade Range' was first used by the Scottish plant collector David Douglas who explored the area in the late 1820s and for whom the Douglas fir is named. Earlier in 1811 British-Canadian map maker and explorer David Thompson had become the first European to navigate the whole Columbia River from source to sea. The stories of both these intrepid men give an insight into what travel was like in the area traversed by the PCT before the advent of maps let alone roads or railways and without any of the backpacking equipment we take for granted. Living off the land and travelling on horseback, on foot and by canoe, often guided by local natives, without whom their journeys would have been impossible, these men were true explorers venturing into an unknown world. I wonder what they would make of the area now.

At Blue Ridge Camp I was just eight miles from the Columbia River and the end of my traverse of Oregon. Many more waterfalls and pools lined the narrow trail as I continued the descent to the little port town of Cascade Locks on the Oregon side of the river. Here I found Wayne and his family in the Cascade Locks Marine Park with a huge and sumptuous picnic spread out on the grass. 'It was great!' I wrote in my journal.

After the feast I wandered over to the park campground to pitch my tent. Here I met Jay J. Johnson, who I'd heard so much about, and a southbound hiker called Robert who told me that Larry was about a week ahead while Scott, Dave and Mark were four days away. They'd told Robert they were planning on 15 miles a day through Washington. I hoped to average more than that – I'd averaged 19 over the last two weeks – so I might yet catch up with them. Jay had met up with Susie and hiked a short way with her but said she was off the trail as she'd been hospitalised with a stomach bug, which was sad news.

The park was on Thunder Island, just offshore of the town, and here I spent my last night in Oregon. At just 150 feet in altitude this was my lowest camp on the PCT. I'd reach the lowest point of all – 140 feet – the next day on the other side of the Columbia River. With just one

State to cross I felt for the first time that the end of the walk was closer than the beginning. I knew though that the PCT had a reputation for toughness in Washington. The easy walking in Northern California and Oregon was over. It was also late August. Summer was fading away in the mountains. Soon the first snows would fall.

The Columbia River and Thunder Island

CHAPTER 5

THE NORTH CASCADES: WASHINGTON

THE COLUMBIA RIVER TO MANNING PARK

August 27 to September 24

484 miles

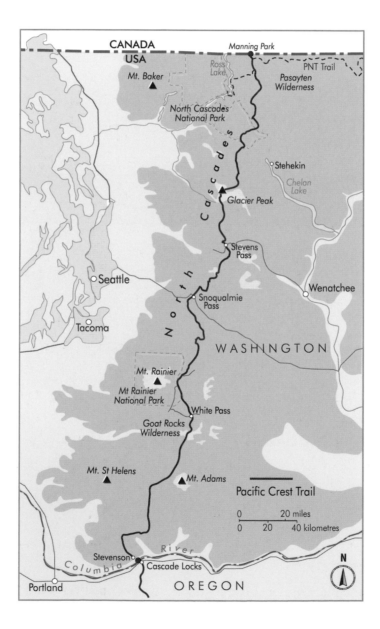

After a breakfast in Cascade Locks I finally left Oregon via the Bridge of the Gods, an impressive cantilever bridge that was built in 1926. The name comes from a Native American legend about a bridge over the river, a legend based in reality as around 1450 A.D. the river was dammed by a landslide that created a land bridge in the vicinity of Cascade Locks. The river backed up behind the dam to create a huge lake before breaking through and washing the debris away. As I walked over the modern bridge I watched ospreys flying over the river and was delighted to see these lovely graceful fish-hawks.

Stepping off the bridge into Washington State I thought about my walk. I was in the last State and had less than 500 miles to go. For the first time I began to think I would reach Canada. Further south I'd become used to people's astonishment on hearing I was walking to Canada. Now they were more amazed that I'd come from Mexico, which was nearly 2,000 miles away. Had I really walked that far? It didn't seem possible.

My first stop in Washington was at the Post Office in the town of Stevenson where I collected my food parcel and my mail, which included the surprise from Warren. This turned out to be the latest edition of the Pacific Crest Club Quarterly containing the letters I'd sent him telling the story of the walk as far as Bullfrog Lake in the High Sierra (my companions had posted the last letter from Independence). I was startled to see my words in print and found reading them very strange. Was I still on the same journey? Today of course PCT walks are documented in online journals and social media on a regular basis and hikers are used to seeing their words and photographs appearing as they go along. Back then this was unimaginable and just seeing my account in print seemed fantastic. It also made me realise just what a long walk this was. This was my 147th day on the trail. It was 92 days since I'd been at Bullfrog Lake. The High Sierra snows felt a long time ago and the Southern California desert and mountains a lifetime away. I'd been a novice in a strange land then. Now I was an experienced and confident long distance walker. Hiking had become my way of life. I couldn't imagine doing anything else. However although I might be much closer to the finish than the start the former was still far enough away for me not to have to think too much about it yet.

I sat in a café reading my words and my mail and then writing letters and postcards. I also bought a copy of *Backpacker* magazine that had a review of lightweight boots, a new category back then. One of the higher rated models was the high-topped version of my shoes. The only negative point, said the tester, was that the stitching had abraded. I had the same problem. The uppers of my shoes were a mix of synthetic and leather panels so there was a great deal of stitching, some of which was coming undone. I didn't think I could complain though, not after the harsh volcanic rocks of the last few weeks. I'd hiked 647 miles in them too. Luckily Stevenson had a shoe repair shop and I had the seams sewn up for just $1.50. Now I hoped they'd make it to Canada. Other hikers had commented on my footwear, which was unusual back then. Most of the day and weekend hikers I met wore fairly hefty leather boots like those I'd started out in. However some other PCT hikers had also changed to lightweight boots or shoes. Jay was hiking in $25 work boots which he'd said didn't last that long but which were cheap and comfortable. My shoes were proving comfortable but I was having problems with my socks. I'd been buying new pairs as I went along and the last two pairs had not been very good. The seams were rough to start with and once they'd been worn for a few days the synthetic material had become fairly harsh too, something washing didn't remove, and they'd quickly developed holes. In Cascade Locks I dumped them and bought two new pairs – the seventh and eighth in total – that I hoped would be more comfortable. Learning from this experience on future walks I put wool socks in my supply boxes so I wasn't reliant on ones I could buy along the way.

The guidebook suggested that the first few days out from the Columbia River were quite tough, as they involved a long ascent back up into the mountains, and also not very interesting. Lured by restaurants and cafes I didn't leave Stevenson until late afternoon and it was well after dark when I reached the Panther Creek Campground after 15 miles of hard-on-the-feet road walking so I just rolled out my groundsheet, got in my sleeping bag and fell asleep. I felt very tired and over-stuffed with food. Although I didn't realise it until the next day I had now walked 2,000 miles.

Panther Creek was only some 800 feet above the Columbia River so I still had a long climb ahead to reach the mountains. I had a heavy pack too, loaded with ten days food and five paperback books. A waterless 17 miles with 4,000 feet of ascent in stifling humidity led from Panther Creek to an unappealing muddy puddle called Sheep Lake, where I camped anyway as I was tired and thirsty, treating the water with purifying tablets. There were some views of huge glacier-clad Mount Adams but otherwise it was not a day to remember.

At Sheep Lake there were mosquitoes and the sky was clouding over. Soon it was raining. At least, I thought, I'm back up in the mountains. The rain continued into the next morning and for the first time on the walk I adopted a backpacking technique from home – light the stove, make another hot drink, open my book and wait in the hope the rain will stop. In this case it didn't quite, just turning to drizzle and a wet white mist by the time I thought I really had to get going. I realised I might have to walk in similar conditions quite often in the days to come as I knew the time for continuous sunny weather had passed and that the Washington Cascades had a wetter more variable climate than the mountains to the south anyway. In September, which was just three days away, the first snows of winter might fall and storms were likely.

At a spot called Blue Lakes the drizzle turned back to real rain so I stopped for lunch in the shelter of a big tree. Jay passed by and told me he was heading for the old Cascade Crest Trail, which was built in the 1930s and which here took a lower route than the PCT (mostly the two coincide with the PCT replacing the older trail), his mind set on reaching Canada as quickly and easily as possible. When the rain eased I set off, sticking to the PCT, only to be caught in a real heavy downpour. All the hills were shrouded in cloud and I saw little. Walking in dense, wet, misty forests continued the next day all the way to a camp by the White Salmon River, which despite its name was just a dry gully where the trail crossed it. A noise of falling water led me to a gushing spring in dense undergrowth fifty yards downstream.

I was just inside the Mount Adams Wilderness now and the next few days looked scenically promising so I was hoping the weather would clear up. And it did. I woke to a clear sky and fine weather that lasted until the evening. The timberline traverse below Mount Adams was excellent. Flowery meadows interspersed with groves of subalpine fir and mountain hemlock gave a soft background to the massive White Salmon Glacier and the steep, fractured icefalls of the Adams Glacier that poured down from the bulky, flat-topped mountain; the white ice flowing in great surges and split and cracked with crevasses. The second highest mountain in Washington 12,281 foot Mount Adams is massive, its spreading bulk making it impressive even though it doesn't have the cone or dome-like summit of other strato-volcanoes. Far to the north I could see wreaths of dirty cumulus clouds around distant peaks but the sky above Mount Adams remained blue. Snowless Mount St. Helens, much closer now, was giving off wisps of steam. I wouldn't see it often again as it lies well to the west of the PCT and I was now passing it by. Beyond St. Helens the white bulk of Mount Rainier could be seen. Both these mountains had disappeared into cloud by late afternoon but I didn't mind as I'd enjoyed the traverse

Mount Adams

below Mount Adams and was delighted to be back at timberline. The walking had been slightly softer and gentler than the trail across Mount Hood, I think because it was just below rather than on the mountain. I passed many scenic camp sites with views of Mount Adams but feeling energetic I pushed on and descended back down into the forest before camping. Just before I did so a deep rich red-brown coloured pine marten with something in its mouth ran across the trail. This was my first sighting of one on the walk and I was very pleased to see it.

From here on, bar a few days in logged areas, the PCT in Washington would be a delight, a magnificent long finale to the walk in the most sustained area of mountain grandeur and wilderness outside of the High Sierra. I was now in the most rugged and continuously mountainous part of the Cascades. I think the Washington section is the main reason for hiking the PCT from Mexico to Canada rather than the other way as it means finishing the walk on a spectacular high (there are good practical reasons as well but given the illogicality of long distance hiking anyway

Entering the Goat Rocks Wilderness
In the Goat Rocks Wilderness

I'd always put aesthetics first). I suspect if I'd gone southwards I'd have found the deserts and lower hills of Southern California made for a low key finish (and this in fact was to happen three years later when I hiked the Continental Divide Trail from Canada to Mexico).

From Mount Adams the PCT climbs into the Goat Rocks Wilderness where, unusually, it actually follows the crest of the hills. This was real mountain walking on rugged, rocky terrain and I relished it. Goat Rocks is an alpine area of jagged, narrow ridges, small glaciers and peaks (Gilbert Peak at 8,201 feet is the highest). This splintered terrain is actually the decaying remnants of an ancient volcano that once rose to over 12,000 feet and was already extinct some 2,000,000 years ago, since when erosion has worn it down to its current state. The name comes from the mountain goats that live on the rocks. I spent two days crossing this exciting and wonderful landscape split by a night spent high in the mountains. I didn't see any goats though.

The traverse of Goat Rocks began with a curving ascent round the Walupt Lake Basin in a mixed forest of dense mountain hemlock and open lodgepole pine plus many Alaska cedars with their distinctive wilted look. The views of the Goat Rocks from this ascent were good but they really opened up on the climb above timberline to 6,460 foot Cispus Pass from where I looked across the deep Klickitat River valley to the barren rock and talus wall of Gilbert Peak. After a descent

151

Ives Peak, Goat Rocks Wilderness
Dana May Yelverton Shelter with Mount Rainier in the distance
Warning sign, Goat Rocks Wilderness

into the Cispus River Basin I climbed back up 1000 feet through glacial run-off washes and dusty scree slopes interspersed with rich alpine flower meadows on the slopes of Old Snowy Mountain to the tiny rough stone Dana May Yelverton Shelter at 7040 feet. The shelter was surrounded by wind and frost stunted four to ten foot high hemlocks and whitebark pine. Leaving my gear in the shelter I climbed to a superb vantage point on the ridge just above it from where there were impressive views of Mounts Rainier, Hood and St. Helens plus the Goat Rocks peaks. Here I sat and watched a fine sunset over permanently frozen Goat Lake after which an almost full moon appeared in the sky. After all the weeks in the forest I felt a sense of euphoria at being back high in the mountains again. A cold wind eventually sent me back down to the shelter where I could see stars through holes in the roof. I noted in my journal that unless it was repaired soon the whole roof would collapse. I guess this never happened as the shelter is now a ruin. I enjoyed my night inside as the walls kept off the wind. I wouldn't have liked it so much if it had rained though.

The next day was one of two very different halves, starting with more superb mountain walking but finishing with getting lost in the forest and having to push hard to reach my next supply point at the White Pass Ski Area. I wasn't actually running out of food so didn't need to be there that day but having decided I could be I was determined enough, or perhaps just pig-headed enough, to keep going. The long, tiring day began with a pretty pink, red and orange dawn that set me up for a grand high-level walk along narrow, winding mountain paths surrounded by jagged rock peaks and grey, debris spattered glaciers. I crossed a 7080 foot saddle, the high point of the PCT in Washington, and then traversed the slopes of Old Snowy Mountain above the shining ice of the Packwood Glacier. Next the trail went round some pinnacles on a narrow ridge between Egg Butte and Elk Pass. A sign warned that there were no passing places for stock on this section of the trail. I was glad I didn't meet any other hikers, let alone horses, as the trail was very narrow and the slopes below steep and rocky. To the north Mount Rainier dominated the view. This was all splendid stuff and very enjoyable but the day was about to change.

From Elk Pass a descent led through stunted three foot high trees into tall subalpine forest and the meadows of the McCall Basin, a flat hanging valley. Here I lost the trail. After a futile hour going round and round the basin trying to find where the trail exited from it I gave up and decided I'd have to bushwhack in as straight a line as possible to a point where I should find the trail again. That resulted in spending another hour stumbling through dense forest and clambering over fallen trees on compass bearings for a mile to Lutz Lake, where I finally stumbled over the trail. This tiring delay turned what should have been a relatively easy day, with plenty of time to reach White Pass before the post office shut, into an arduous slog. It was midday when I reached Lutz Lake and I still had 11 miles and a 2000 foot climb to go. I knew from previous places that the post office could shut at 4 p.m. and would certainly be shut at 5. I hammered up the climb, paused for a look down at beautiful pale blue Shoe Lake then continued on a pleasant traverse of the rough but scenic slopes of Hogback Ridge before racing down through the forest to reach White Pass at 4.45 p.m. feeling hot, exhausted and very thirsty only to discover that I needn't have rushed at all. The Kracker Barrel Grocery Store was also the post office and the owner had a very relaxed and friendly attitude to PCT hikers. I could have collected my mail any time during the evening. Probably dehydrated from pushing on without bothering to stop to drink as well as very tired and overheated I felt faint in the very hot store so grabbed some cold cans of Coke and sat outside to drink them. In the register I discovered that Wayne had been here the day

Mount Rainier rising above the forest

before and that Scott and Dave were still four days ahead. All three were planning on reaching Canada in eighteen days' time. An unpleasant entry from a PCT hiker I'd never met attacked Scott, Dave, Larry and me, saying we couldn't have gone through the High Sierra as it had been impossible to do so. I'd seen this comment from him in other registers but hadn't responded. This time, fed up with the suggestion I was a liar, I wrote some choice words and the next day sent him a postcard asking why he'd been saying this. I never had a reply. I could only guess that as he hadn't gone through the High Sierra he needed to think it had been impassable. The long day ended sleeping under the stars on the White Pass Campground beside dragonfly haunted Leech Lake.

Noisy birds woke me at dawn. A whole flock of gray jays were in camp but it was a few raucous Stellar's jays that were making all the noise. Beautiful to look at these birds have a very harsh and ugly call. There was a pair of hairy woodpeckers drumming in the trees too and an American robin bobbing over the ground. The sky was a leaden grey and soon it was raining steadily. Without ever consciously deciding to do so I had a rest day, my first since Ashland thirty days before. I had been feeling weary at the end of recent days and probably needed the rest. The grocery had a laundromat and a shower available to PCT hikers so I was able to do some necessary washing of my clothes and myself. I spent the day alternating between the store and the Continental Café just across the road in the ski lodge. Mike, the manager of the store, was a mountaineer, backpacker and skier and I had a long interesting chat with him about the PCT and the Cascades. Jay arrived at lunchtime – I'd thought he was ahead of

Shoe Lake

me – soon followed by other hikers out for the Labor Day weekend. I sent a postcard to Scott and Dave at Stehekin, the last supply point before the end of the trail, in case I didn't catch them up. Although Jay was the only other PCT hiker here I found that reading the register, which was full of entries from those who'd skipped sections and come up here weeks and months before, made me feel I was part of a community of PCT hikers heading for Canada for the first time since those long ago pre-High Sierra days. How many, I wondered, had already reached Canada.

Mike offered the loft above the store to sleep in so as it was still raining I moved in there with three hikers heading for the Goat Rocks Wilderness. The rain and cloud meant I never saw the full moon that night, the last one of the walk. I would be back home for the next one. Slowly the walk was drawing to a close. I still had three weeks left though and some tough and spectacular terrain to cross.

Before leaving White Pass I weighed my pack. With six days' supplies it came to 63lbs, which the pack handled well. I'd grown used to it now and was quite happy with the design. The rain had stopped but the clouds were still low, as they remained all day so there were no views. After all the rain the trail for the first ten miles was incredibly muddy and slippery, made worse by all the horses that had been and were using it – six passed me as I plodded along. I also saw dozens of backpackers out on this last holiday weekend of the summer. The condition of the trail improved in the afternoon and the walking became more enjoyable though the mountains remained hidden. After twenty miles and 2,700 feet of ascent I camped at Twin Lakes on the edge of Mount Rainier National Park. The walk had taken just 71/2 hours. I hadn't hiked this quickly for quite a while. I'd needed that day off. Of course the lack of views and the damp, chilly air had also kept me moving briskly but I suspect I'd have stopped sooner if I hadn't rested at White Pass. In camp I noticed that the stitching on my shoes was coming apart again. Would they last another three weeks? (They did, just). I was also having problems with condensation in my single-skin tent due to the very humid weather and had to be very careful not to brush against the damp walls.

The PCT only just touches the eastern edge of Mount Rainier National Park but the country it passes through outside the park is just as majestic and gives splendid views of Mount Rainier. This country is now protected in the William O. Douglas and Norse Peak Wilderness Areas, though these weren't designated until two years after my walk. The centrepiece of the whole area is Mount Rainier, the highest peak in the Cascades at 14,411 feet, which towers above the forest, dominating the view for many, many miles. Rainier is also the most heavily glaciated mountain in the 48 lower states with 26 named glaciers covering around 36 square miles. It's still an active volcano, last erupting in the late nineteenth century. The first Europeans to see the mountain were the members of the British naval expedition led by Captain George Vancouver that explored the coast here in 1792. Rainier was named by Vancouver (he named many places in the area) after a British admiral who, as so often in such cases, never even saw the mountain that bore his name (Mount Everest is the most famous example of this Imperial naming). The mountain already had a local name of course, Tacoma. The meaning of this is unclear but the favourites are 'mother of waters' or 'snow-covered mountain', which both make sense. For many years the mountain was known by both names but in 1890 Rainier was made the official one. There is an ongoing campaign to revert to the local name, which would seem far more appropriate than that of a naval officer from a far off country. The national park was created in 1899, the fifth such park in the USA.

Rainier is not an easy mountain to climb due to the glaciers and the steepness. The first recorded ascent was in 1870 by Hazard Stevens (wonderful name for a mountaineer!) and Phillmon Van Trump. John Muir climbed it in 1888 and described his ascent dramatically in his book *Steep Trails*. Although impressed he doesn't sound absolutely certain of the joys of the ascent writing: 'The view we enjoyed from the summit could hardly be surpassed in sublimity and grandeur; but one feels far from home so high in the sky, so much so that one is inclined to guess that, apart from the acquisition of knowledge and the exhilaration of climbing, more pleasure is to be found at the foot of the mountains than on their tops. Doubly happy, however, is the man to whom lofty mountain tops are within reach, for the lights that shine there illumine all that lies below.' Camp Muir, a refuge on the mountain used as a base camp for ascents, was built in 1921 in memory of John Muir.

I wasn't planning on climbing Mount Rainier, an alpine expedition that would have meant renting climbing equipment and booking with a guide. I didn't have the time anyway. I was happy merely to gaze on the great mountain as I walked past it in the woods and meadows, finding pleasure, as Muir suggested, at the foot of the mountain. The morning at Twin Lakes was cold enough for me to wear my warm hat for the first time in months, a reminder that the seasons were changing.

This was the only time I'd been in a popular area on a holiday weekend and I was amazed at the number of people about, especially near Chinook Pass, where the trail crossed an access road into the park that was lined with parked cars. Either side of this busy highway the trails were packed with day hikers all enjoying the dramatic and beautiful scenery. Many of them asked me what I was doing – I didn't look like a day hiker or a weekend backpacker! The strangest conversation was with a woman who on hearing my accent said she could tell English wasn't my first language and she'd try and guess where I was from. After a pause she triumphantly came up with an answer. Belgium! I could only guess she'd run through accents she knew – French, German, Italian, Spanish maybe – and come up with one she didn't know and assumed that must be mine. She was very surprised when I told her I was English. Another woman decided I must be hungry – I was very skinny – and insisted I take some fresh plums, tomato, cucumber and a sandwich. This

Near Chinook Pass

was more than I needed or could eat at the time but she wouldn't accept a refusal. Talking to all the people did take time but their friendliness and genuine interest was heartening.

In total contrast to the previous day the weather was fine and there were superb views all day. The trail wound along ridges, across meadows and below crags. Much of the time it followed a narrow crest with only a few trees so there were constant views. Those back to Goat Rocks and Mount Adams were excellent, those of Mount Rainier breath-taking. There were many attractive timberline lakes too, all of them surrounded by tents. By Sheep Lake I met a backpacker walking from Snoqualmie Pass, my next supply point, to White Pass who had hiked the whole PCT in 1975. There was no snow in the High Sierra in May that year he told me. He'd met Scott, Dave and Mark and said they were going to have a rest day at Snoqualmie. That meant they'd be leaving the day before I planned on getting there. Maybe I will catch up with them I thought. I wasn't going to hike faster to do so but it would be nice to meet them again before the end of the trail.

From Sheep Lake the steepest climb of the day led up to a notch called Sourdough Gap from where another narrow trail undulated along the crest of the hills to Big Crow Basin. There was a shelter half a mile off the trail here but I didn't visit it as I could see smoke rising and hear horses and thought it might well be full. Instead I camped in the woods by the trail.

The hills became more rounded and wooded as I left Rainier and its environs behind and the next day was mostly a lengthy descent on the dwindling Cascade crest down to Government Meadows where there was a good cabin at Camp Ulrich. In stormy weather I'd probably have taken advantage of the shelter but it was sunny and still early so I continued the descent. Then, just when I thought I'd be descending right out of the mountains, the trail turned uphill for a 900 foot climb that led up 5754 foot Blowout Mountain, passing about 100 feet below the summit. Succulent sweet huckleberries grew beside the trail and I ate handfuls of these as I climbed. The above timberline trail led to Arch Rock Shelter, which I thought could be useful in a storm (it no longer exists), and had excellent views back to cloud-swathed Mount Rainier. More exciting though was the sight of the rough, jagged peaks beyond Snoqualmie Pass amongst which I would soon be hiking in the enticingly named Alpine Lakes Wilderness. A final descent down steep slopes led to a camp on a flat bench on the steep slopes of Blowout Mountain. A shallow muddy pond full of tadpoles and little frogs looked to be the only water but a search in the undergrowth revealed the outlet stream, which was clear of mud and amphibians.

I was now 35 miles from Snoqualmie Pass, which should have been an easy two-day pleasant walk in the forest. This wasn't to be however. Firstly I lengthened the distance by 4 miles by taking the wrong trail from my camp in thick mist, flurries of rain and a gusty wind. Only when I came on a sign did I realise I was on the Blowout Mountain Trail and not the PCT. So back up I went to start again. Much worse however was what was to follow when I finally escaped from Blowout Mountain – a horrible day of clear-cuts and logging, a day that was probably the worst of the whole walk. Not that it was hard or exhausting or dangerous. It wasn't. It was soul-destroying, which was much worse. There were roads everywhere and I could hear chainsaws and bulldozers echoing across the devastated forest. Virtually the whole area had been clear-cut for many miles. The trail was a muddy mess as it wound through the tree stumps and debris. This was a huge tree slaughterhouse. Just wanting to escape this blasted terrain I walked as fast as I could, sweating heavily in the hot sun. Why was I here? Because I wanted to hike all of the PCT of course. It certainly wasn't for enjoyment. I didn't expect to see anyone else and so was surprised when I saw a backpacker coming towards me. We stopped in the midst of the devastation for a chat. Paul was a PCT hiker naturally – no-one else would walk here. He wasn't a thru-hiker though but was walking a week long section each summer. It had taken him four years to reach this point. At that rate it would take another 28 years to reach Mexico! He told me that an Australian PCT hiker called Ron Ellis was about a day ahead and just a few hours away was Greg Poirier, a hiker I'd last heard of in Weldon where I'd been told he'd set off solo into the High Sierra.

Overleaf: Mount Rainier

Sure enough I soon caught up with Greg and hiked with him for the rest of the day. For once I was very glad of company as conversation was a distraction from the appalling mess around us. Greg had started the trail on March 12, three weeks before me, and had indeed set off into the High Sierra. However he'd soon retreated on discovering how much snow there was. Determined to do a continuous hike and not wanting to trudge up the road in Owens Valley he'd headed east across that valley and then hiked along the White Mountains that paralleled the Sierra Nevada. He'd been inspired to do this by Colin Fletcher's *The Thousand-Mile Summer* as that was the route Fletcher had taken. This was the book that inspired my walk too of course and we enjoyed discussing it. I thought heading for the White Mountains had been imaginative and adventurous and felt that Greg was a backpacker after my own heart. Meeting him restored my morale on a day when it was declining rapidly.

Finding a campsite in this trashed land proved difficult. There was nowhere clear enough of tangled branches to pitch a tent. We thought Stirrup Lake might have space on its shores but the trail there had been destroyed and a giant latticework of felled trees waiting to be removed blocked our way. Eventually, just as dark was falling, we found two bumpy but bare spots either side of the trail. Mosquitoes and midges ended the unpleasant day.

The sound of heavy logging operations starting up near camp woke us early the next morning. 'It'll be a relief to get to Snoqualmie and out of this mess', I wrote in my journal over breakfast. I was not happy. This was the only section of trail I wanted to run away from. The situation has only worsened since then according to recent hikers as more areas have been clear-but. It's arguable that the 40 miles south of Snoqualmie Pass is the worst section of the whole PCT.

The vandalised forest continued much of the way to Snoqualmie Pass and again we tried to distract ourselves with conversation and fast walking. By 1.30 p.m. we were looking down on Interstate 90 roaring across the Cascades as we descended past ski tows to the pass. Snoqualmie had the usual collection of ski lodge, café, store and post office that were found at most high road crossings in the Cascades. I collected my penultimate food parcel and did the usual chores. Would I really only do this once more? I was pleased that the store had paperback books and camera film as I was running short of both and especially pleased that amongst the books was mountaineer Fred Beckey's classic *The Challenge of the North Cascades* about his vast number of ascents in the range, and Stephen Arno's *Northwest Trees*, which would tell me

Greg Poirier approaching Snoqualmie Pass

more about the wonderful trees of the Cascades. I'd read both over the next few weeks. In the trail register I found a message from Scott and Dave saying they planned on reaching Canada on the 24th. That was my finish date too so seeing them again was becoming more and more likely.

On the Commonwealth Campground in Snoqualmie Pass I found Ron Ellis, the Australian hiker, who said he was glad to finally meet me as he was getting fed up with people asking him if he was the English PCT hiker. I'd been asked if I was the Australian or English hiker quite a few times in recent weeks by people who assured me our accents were identical, something that puzzled us both. Ron was a section hiker, that is someone who was doing the PCT in bits. He hadn't started until May 13th and had then done Campo to Acton before travelling up to Belden and heading north. He hoped to hike the High Sierra and the Mohave Desert after he reached Canada though he knew the first winter snow might prevent him going through the former.

163

He told he me he'd been distracted by the volcanoes and had climbed every one of them since Lassen Peak, taking many days off the trail to do so. I was impressed.

So far I hadn't lost a single day due to the weather. This changed at Snoqualmie Pass. I woke to heavy rain and thick mist. The forecast was for snow above 6,500 feet. Weekenders retreating from the north confirmed this. With steep ascents and narrow trails in big mountains to come sitting out the storm seemed wise. Beyond the pass the trail climbed up into the North Cascades, the most alpine, steep and mountainous section of the whole PCT and which stretched all the way to Canada. The bad weather continued all day with sheets of rain and swirling clouds sweeping through the pass. My retreat was to the café where I spent the day writing letters and talking to PCT hikers as they drifted in during the day. As at the start of the trail the finish was bringing thru-hikers together and by the end of the day seven of us were there. Of the others I was most surprised to meet Ron DiBaccio, who I'd last seen in Cabazon with his girlfriend Cheryl nearly five months ago. Ron wasn't surprised to see me as he'd been following me since Northern California determined to catch me up. He'd managed to do so now only because of an unfortunate injury. A few days earlier he'd hurt his ankle badly and been rescued and brought down on horseback from Arch Rock Shelter. He'd come here to recuperate for a few days. Not wanting to tackle the snow in the High Sierra he and Cheryl had gone to the coast but he'd returned later to start the hike again further north. Ron had turned up with Robert, who I'd met in Cascade Locks with Jay who himself arrived not long afterwards.

Rain poured down all night and into the next morning. I delayed departure and spent a few hours chatting to Ron DiBaccio and the other hikers. Ron Ellis was the only one to set off in the rain. By the afternoon the rain had stopped though the cloud was still low. Not wanting to delay any longer I started out. The others were going to wait a little longer. Two hikers who were descending told me there was snow on the trail not far above. I encountered the first of it at 5,000 feet – a couple of inches of wet snow sitting on top of mud and making the trail very slippery. Care was needed to negotiate the narrow trail safely as it wound round steep slopes above deep valleys. This was not a place to fall off the trail. My load didn't help. I was carrying 11 days supplies, the last time I would carry this much, and my pack was top heavy and a little unstable. The landscape was really dramatic even though I couldn't see the summits and I very quickly felt as though I was back in big mountains. With such a late start and much ascent to do I only made seven and a half miles before camping beside Gravel Lake. This wasn't the weather for walking in the dark. I fell asleep hoping it wouldn't freeze as ice would make the trail really treacherous. For the first time I realised that the weather could stop me finishing the trail. Summer was over, autumn was here and winter was on the way. In my journal I wrote 'every

Snow on the trail above Snoqualmie Pass

good day now I'm going to do 20+ miles. I want to reach Canada before the winter really sets in'.

Thankfully there was no frost overnight. However I did wake to rain and an inch of soft wet snow covering the tent and the ground. This snow was thawing rapidly and I was soon camped in a rapidly spreading puddle. A very wet day followed. I wore all my clothes and got soaked to the skin, my well-worn waterproof clothing no longer coping with the weather. It was so wet I doubt anything would have kept me dry. The air was harshly cold and I felt chilled. In the heavy rain there were no views. From the steepness of the terrain I guessed the scenery was spectacular. As I climbed the snow on the trail grew deeper and I was glad I still had my ice axe as in places the trail was again narrow and often above steep drops. Carrying the ice axe through the gentle snow free terrain of Northern California and Oregon had seemed foolish but luckily something had stopped me sending it home.

I left the snow for a descent into the Park Lakes Basin and then down 66 switchbacks (according to the guidebook, I didn't count them – they did seem endless) to a torrent called Lemah Creek by which I camped. The rain had continued pouring down and streams had burst their banks in many places. At times the trail became a stream itself. My feet were sodden, there now being

165

several holes in the tattered uppers of my shoes, not that I thought they'd have kept me dry in this even when new. Inside the tent it was damp and steamy but still quite cosy compared with outside. I wondered though how many days I'd be able to cope with such wet conditions before my gear was just too damp for me to stay warm and dry enough not to risk hypothermia. The storm had lasted for three days now with barely a let-up in the rain. I was glad I had a waterproof bivi bag to pull over my down sleeping bag. I hadn't used this much but now it was essential for keeping my sleeping bag reasonably dry.

At 3 a.m. in the morning I woke briefly and looked out. The rain had stopped and I could see a few stars through the trees. Hopeful the storm was over I drifted back to sleep, waking at dawn to silence. No rain was falling on the tent. There was a pool of water at one end of the tent though, caused by condensation running down the walls, and the foot of my sleeping bag was damp even though it was inside the bivi bag – I guess the pressure had forced water through the latter or the waterproofing was punctured, even a tiny pinhole could let water in. I needed to dry out my gear soon or life would become very uncomfortable.

In the tent porch I discovered a hole in a bag of trail mix. Some small creature had crept in and had a snack. I ate my own breakfast from inside the sleeping bag then donned my wet clothes, at which point the rain started again. Reluctant to leave the shelter of the tent I decided a second breakfast was a good idea and passed the morning reading *The Challenge of the North Cascades* – an apt title – and smearing glue on the tears in my shoes in the hope this would at least slow down the deterioration. As I sat there Jay and Robert turned up. They'd been camped just a quarter of a mile away. After they left I finally packed up as the sky was starting to clear and the rain had stopped. The damp air was chilly but I soon warmed up on the long slow climb up the side of Escondido Ridge. As the weather improved so the views opened up and I could finally see I really was in the middle of some spectacular and rugged mountain country. Across the deep Lemah Valley the hanging glaciers of Lemah Peak glistened in the sunshine. During the ascent I heard a couple of gunshots and shortly afterwards met two hunters with rifles who told me the autumn hunting season had opened the previous day. This was something I would now have to take into account. My clothing was mostly dark and sombre and designed to blend in. Only my blue pack stood out. I wished I had something red or orange to wear. I didn't want to be mistaken for a deer.

At the top of the climb was a pleasant rocky cirque with a small pool at its heart. Here I found Jay and Robert having a break. Jay had spread his damp gear over the sun warmed rocks to dry, a great idea I immediately copied. The sun was hot and everything was soon steaming merrily. Once his gear was dry Jay strode off leaving Robert and me to follow soon afterwards. The trail continued across the upper part of Escondido Ridge with views of over Escondido and Waptus Lakes to magnificent snow-capped peaks. On one a huge easy angled rock slab that I estimated was at least a 1000 feet long reached almost to the summit, a dramatic feature that drew the cye. Finally I was seeing the magnificent peaks of the North Cascades. The day ended with a long, easy angled descent down what seemed interminable switchbacks to the Waptus River by which we camped. This was to be the pattern through the North Cascades – long climbs to ridges and high passes followed by long descents into deep forested valleys followed almost immediately by the next climb. Along with the section in Yosemite the North Cascades had the most ascent and descent per mile on the PCT. I realised too that the steep slopes meant I had to think in advance about camp sites. There were rarely any flat areas during the ascents or descents so starting one late in the day was unwise.

Talking to Robert that evening I learned that he and Jay were having worse problems with the rain than me. Jay, said Robert, had a non-waterproof single-skin tent so to keep the rain out he had to throw his plastic groundsheet over it which then meant ground water would soak through the tent's porous floor. Jay's pack was leaking too and he didn't have a waterproof cover or liner for it. Used to the damp British climate I was using a waterproof cover over my pack along with water-resistant stuffsacks inside so my gear stayed reasonably dry. Robert's problem was the size of his tent rather than its performance. With tiny hoops at each end it only rose a foot above the ground, which meant that whilst he could stay dry lying inside he couldn't do anything such as cook or sit up. To try and overcome this he rigged the space blanket he'd brought for emergencies over the front to make a porch. It didn't look very effective. My tent was roomy and waterproof and had a large porch in which I could store wet gear and cook. Robert's mini-tent was undoubtedly much lighter but in stormy weather I'd much rather have the extra weight. Sitting in the tent in the rain I was warm and comfortable and didn't feel restricted or claustrophobic.

Robert was still sitting in his hooped mini-tent/tarp rig when I left early the next morning, keen to get going as the sun was shining. Slowly the forest opened out to give views of the rock tower of Cathedral Peak. I met some hikers and horse riders descending the trail who gave me news of PCT hikers ahead including Larry who'd been at Stevens Pass, the next road crossing, looking ill from a stomach upset several days earlier. I hope it was nothing serious. (I never heard of Larry again on the trail but later I found out that he had completed the PCT).

A climb led to Cathedral Pass after which there was a dipping and rising traverse across the steep glaciated slopes of 7899 foot Mount Daniel to Deception Pass. A notice beside the trail advised following a detour as a glacial stream up ahead was dangerous to ford. The hikers I'd met earlier had told me to ignore this as the creek was easily crossed on logs. I did and it was. Throughout the day there many views of the waterfalls, cliffs and hanging valleys on the steep mountainsides, a wonderful vertical world. Steep, there was a word that summed up the North Cascades. Beyond Deception Pass I had the best view of long glacier clad 7,960 foot Mount Daniel, the highest peak in the Alpine Lakes Wilderness, looking very dramatic with big cumulus clouds towering up behind it. From Deception Lakes I took the old abandoned Cascade Crest Trail over Surprise Gap to Glacier Lake as it was almost 2 miles and a few hundred feet of ascent shorter than the PCT and I could see no reason to prefer the latter. Why the two trails diverge here for a short while I couldn't imagine. From the bootprints in the mud it looked as though all the hikers in front of me had gone this way too.

Initially the rough, steep, decaying old trail was worth taking for the views back to massive Mac Peak above Deceptions Lakes. The real reward came at Surprise Gap though with a superb view over Glacier Lake to the distant white cone of 10,525 foot Glacier Peak, the next stratovolcano. However unlike the range to the south the Cascades here were not wooded hills only occasionally rising above timberline with the giant stratovolcanoes widely spaced in a line amongst them but a rugged alpine mountain range with glaciers, cliffs and rock peaks amongst which there were also occasional volcanoes. For the first time since the High Sierra I felt as though I was walking day after day in real mountain country. This continued for the remainder of the walk, making the last fortnight wonderful. Here in the Alpine Lakes Wilderness the final glory of the PCT was beginning.

From Surprise Gap I descended the steep boulder strewn trail to Glacier Lake where I camped. I'd walked 22 miles and climbed 4,000 feet and felt fine. The day had been splendid and my gear was dry. The walk felt like it was properly back under way after the disturbance of the storm.

September 14th dawned beautifully clear. I was delighted as it was my 33rd birthday. I'd have hated spending it in a storm seeing nothing (that has happened!) or even worse in an ugly despoiled area. On this day both weather and scenery were splendid. The clarity of the views was superb as a cold dry east wind blew all day preventing any heat haze from forming and keeping the humidity low. Trap Pass gave a good view of the rock towers of Thunder Mountain after which there was a long gentle descent through slowly declining hills to ski lifts at Stevens Pass where, unusually, there was no ski resort or store, just the highway. Across the pass the trail soon disappeared back into the forest where it stayed, with just one good view of the rock peak of Lichtenburg Mountain across Valhalla Lake, all the way to Janus Lake where there was a rather decrepit open-fronted log shelter called Janice Cabin. Here I found Jay and Ron Ellis and, as I soon discovered, many cheeky mice that scurried over the floor and tried to get into our packs. Jay and Ron had bagged the small sleeping platform so I set up my bed on the floor. I did have a comfortable self-inflating mat though whilst Ron only had a thin piece of closed cell foam and Jay nothing at all. We hung our food from nails in the cabin walls to keep it safe from the rodents. I lay in my sleeping bag looking out at a brilliant clear starry sky. There'll be a frost tonight, I thought, before I fell asleep. It had been a good birthday.

Sure enough the ground outside the cabin was white at dawn. The sun soon rose though and a warm day followed. The changing colours gave the lie to the illusion that it was still summer though; reds and browns were beginning to predominate amongst the undergrowth and along creek banks. It was an up and down sort of day over pleasant rocky hills with good views of distant mountains, especially, again, Glacier Peak which had a large cloud curving dramatically over the summit. Ron had set off before me (and Jay before him) but I caught up with him sitting on a hillside admiring the splendid view. Close by was impressive 9415 foot Mount Stuart while to the south could be seen the peaks around Snoqualmie Pass and big, white Mount Rainier which seemed to be floating above the forests. Ron and I then hiked together for the rest of the day past pleasant lakes and through wooded cirques and up steep slopes to a shoulder of Skykomish Peak where we stopped to eat some delicious blueberries before traversing below the summit in soft evening light and then descending to pretty Lake Sally Ann where we found Jay already camped. The view over the lake was lovely and I noted in my journal 'this is the best site in quite a while'. Mostly I was camping in forests with no views as the steep terrain of the mountains here didn't lend themselves to high camps.

I woke to a beautiful soft dawn. To the south the dark-edged peaks were rose-tinted. The day was magnificent. Again a cold wind, this time from the northeast, kept the air clear, giving a sharp-etched look to the mountains. I thought it the best light since the High Sierra. The trail led under Skykomish Peak and then around treeless slopes covered with red and purple berry bushes to White Pass and Red Pass. Ahead was the glaring almost painful white of Glacier Peak. From Red Pass we had a stupendous view of a vast array of rugged glacier-covered peaks. The 756 glaciers of the North Cascades make up nearly half the glaciers in the USA outside of Alaska. From Red Pass it looked like it with big glaciers and snowfields visible on almost every mountain.

Ron and I parted on Red Pass as he was leaving the PCT to meet some friends for an ascent of Glacier Peak. I'd enjoyed hiking with him but was, as usual, quite happy to be on my own. Saying farewell to Ron I left the pass for a descent down a wide glaciated scenic valley. The day ended with a somewhat reluctant entry into some really dense almost claustrophobic feeling woods by White Chuck Creek. I wanted to be in the sunshine and to see the mountains! After crossing many creeks I found a campsite by one of them, Glacier Creek, that did have a good view.

I was now in the Glacier Peak Wilderness and approaching the magnificent mountain itself, undoubtedly one of the most beautiful on the PCT, and also one of the most remote of the stratovolcanoes. Of all the regions of the PCT this was one I immediately wanted to return to and spend more time in (as I did many years later when I made an autumn circuit of Glacier Peak). From the Glacier Creek camp I climbed up to Fire Creek Pass, a tremendous viewpoint for Glacier Peak and for the vast spread of the North Cascades. Below the pass I reached a fine cirque that held lovely partially frozen Mica Lake. There followed a leg-pounding, steep, long switchback descent through the forest to glacial, avalanche prone Milk Creek. As I descended I could see the trail switchbacking straight back up the other side of the canyon for 1900 feet. The straight line distance to the other side of the narrow canyon was short but the trail distance was long. Beautiful this wilderness might be, it was also rugged and tough. The bridge over Milk Creek had been wrecked, by flood or avalanche, but the water was shallow so fording it was no problem. (In 2003 more serious flooding destroyed a long section of the trail in this area and the PCT had to be rerouted. The trail wasn't repaired until 2011). The 2 1/2 mile long ascent began straight after the crossing. It only took an hour and a quarter but it seemed longer as I was getting tired and it was very hot. From the top of the climb there were more good views

The North Cascades from Fire Creek Pass
Ron Ellis on Red Pass

including to the northwest where I could see what could only be distant Mount Baker, the last stratovolcano before Canada. 10,778 foot Mount Baker lies well to the west of the PCT and isn't visible from many places along it so I was pleased at this view. I was to see it much more closely when I hiked the Pacific Northwest Trail in 2010 as this crosses its slopes.

Camp was down in the forest by the Suiattle River after another steep switchbacking descent. I was deep in the forest here, surrounded by huge and impressive Douglas firs. After all this time the forests could still surprise and delight me. Here these ancient old growth trees, some of which could be over a thousand years old, thrived on the damp climate and grew to massive size. Moss and lichen hung from the branches and there was rich undergrowth below the trees even though the sun rarely reached the forest floor for long due to the thick high canopy. There were many fallen trees, also covered with moss and lichen. There was an air of timelessness in the quiet sombre forest, a feeling of slowness and stillness.

Before I camped I passed a group of cheerful hunters and their horses. I went on until I could no longer hear them then camped just off the trail. Later in the evening I was sitting in the tent after dark reading by candlelight when I was startled by a rifle barrel poking through the open tent door. The hunter waving it just wanted to know the time and whether I'd seen any other hunters. I was happy to direct him to the party I'd passed but I did wonder how the jumpy hiker who'd displayed his gun to me on the slopes of Mount Hood would have reacted to having a rifle pointed at him. I was initially too startled to be alarmed and the hunter did quickly speak so I knew he was friendly. Unsure where he was in the dark I don't think he even realised he'd pointed his rifle at me or intended to do so. It just happened to be in his hand.

This was a well-used site and the local mice were obviously used to campers as they were very bold. One of them ran all over my shoes, garbage, pans and pack, examining each closely and coming within a few inches of me completely unbothered by my presence or the light from my torch. It seemed to have an unhealthy fascination for my sweaty socks and spent rather a long time sniffing them. Remembering the trail mix that had been nibbled at a previous camp I hung my food bag, which was fairly empty now, from a tree branch. As usual since the mosquitoes had stopped being a problem I slept with the tent door wide open. I woke suddenly in the middle of the night with a sharp pain in my head. A mouse was tugging at a strand of my hair! I sat up and it raced away. Not wanting such a shock again I zipped the door shut. I'd survived rattlesnake country and had no problems with bears. I wasn't expecting to be molested by a mouse.

The following day saw the start of my last week on the PCT. I didn't want to think about finishing yet though. I still had over 100 miles of challenging high mountain wilderness to enjoy. I also had one more supply point, at Stehekin on Lake Chelan, which was ten miles off the trail but could be reached by a shuttle bus provided by the North Cascades National Park, which I would enter very soon. As I was running low on food I was keen to reach Stehekin as soon as possible. From the Suiattle River I climbed to Suiattle Pass and superb views of aptly named Fortress Mountain and Glacier Peak where Ron should be making his ascent. The crystalline and metamorphic rocks of the North Cascades give them a distinctive look very different to the mountains further south and Fortress Mountain typified this. The mountainsides along the trail were beautiful with bright autumn tints of red, brown and yellow. I knew that soon they would be covered with snow.

Twice during the day I came on brand new sections of trail that weren't in the guidebook or on Warren's maps. Signs pointed along these as now being the PCT. The first led more directly to Suiattle Pass than the old route, the second went up and around two superb rock-girt cirques below Plummer and Sitting Bull Mountains before descending to the South Fork of Agnes Creek. Here the old and new PCTs reconnected and there was a long gentle descent beside the creek in its deepening canyon. There was just one view down into the gorge through which the big creek crashed but otherwise the ravine was hidden. The South Fork joined the West Fork down in the forest and here I met a porcupine which tried without success to climb a tree when it saw me but failed to get any grip on the bark. I watched it a short while then walked on, leaving the creature in peace.

Late in the day I arrived at a backcountry campsite called Five Mile Camp, deep in majestic forest. As I approached I could see figures and heard voices that soon became very familiar. On hearing me approach they turned towards me and we all let out whoops of glee. After 12 weeks and 1400 miles I'd finally met up with Scott and Dave, just 100 miles from the Canadian border, along with Mark, who'd been with them for several weeks. We had a grand reunion, all trying to tell our tales at once. I was delighted to see them as I'd just about given up hope of doing so. Too tired to pitch the tent I slept outside only to be disturbed several times by a deer that kept approaching me noisily then backing off when I shone a light at it.

The next morning it was just a short walk down to the roadhead to catch the shuttle bus to Stehekin. We were in the little settlement, which is strung out along Lake Chelan, before noon. Stehekin is unusual as there is no road access. It can only be reached by hiking, horseback, boat or plane. The shuttle bus runs 10 miles to the trailhead but that's it for road transport. Stehekin has a post office, store, cafe and the Purple Point Campground where we stayed. As it was a Sunday we couldn't collect our mail so we sat round eating and talking. There were many stories to tell, especially when Jay arrived and joined us. A last gathering of PCT hikers, I thought.

The next morning I collected my last food parcel, my last set of maps and a mass of birthday cards and then sat on the dock watching float planes fly in and out along with the ferry that plies the lake and planning my supplies for the last days of the walk. It really was nearly over. I chatted to the park ranger who told me the forecast for the next few days was mixed. Late in the afternoon I caught the bus back up to the roadhead at High Bridge where there was a good shelter that I shared with Scott, Dave and Mark. Canada was 88 miles away. Mexico around 2,400. It was hard to believe. I really had walked all that way.

From High Bridge the first fifteen miles of the trail were in the North Cascades National Park. The PCT only cuts across a small corner of this magnificent park but its tangled alpine peaks are in view from it for much of the last 100 miles. Most of the park is managed as wilderness and much is pretty inaccessible due to the extremely steep and rugged terrain, the dense old growth forests and the more than 300 glaciers.

We left High Bridge together but I soon pulled ahead. The others were planning on 61/2 days to the finish, I hoped to do it in 4. Whilst it had been very enjoyable meeting up with the others and I'd been especially glad to see Scott and Dave again I wanted to finish on my own. As at the start of this great adventure I wanted to feel the PCT was mine. And I wanted to relish these last few days in the wilderness and experience them as deeply as I could. I was restless too. The realisation that I was almost certainly going to make it to Canada suddenly became very real and I was urged on by excitement and the nagging fear that something might go wrong at the last minute.

The day was spent mainly in forest, with some views of rocky peaks, on a long very gradual ascent by Bridge Creek to Rainy Pass and the North Cascades Highway, the last road I would cross. The trees and the rich vegetation were lovely. The highlight of the day though was a close encounter with a black bear. I rounded a bend in the trail and there it was about thirty feet away and walking towards me. For a second or two we both froze and then the bear ran off, uphill, rippling through the undergrowth and brushing aside bushes as though they did not exist. I was surprised by the fluidity and grace of movement of such an apparently bulky and ponderous animal. I realised too why the advice given by bear experts is never to run away. There was no way I could have outrun it. This was the closest I'd come to one of these prime symbols of wilderness and I was glad to have had such a close encounter.

At Rainy Pass I left the North Cascades National Park and climbed through the forest to camp by Porcupine Creek. The ascent continued the next morning up out of the trees and through meadows and rock fields to the narrow notch of Cutthroat Pass and a sweeping view of the North Cascades. The splendid vistas continued all day. From the pass a long traverse took me past arid-looking rock peaks across several scree and talus slopes. I was on the east side of the Cascades here and in the rain shadow of the big mountains to the west so it was much drier than most of the region. Of the many soaring peaks I could see from the pass the rock pyramids

Trail sign near Rainy Pass
Cutthroat Pass

of Tower Mountain and Mount Hardy stood out. The bushes beside the trail were red and yellow, their colours amplified by the bright yellow needles of the alpine larches (a final new tree!) and the yellowish Golden Horn granodiorite rock. It was all wonderful and my heart sang. I felt I could walk through such country forever. Another traverse round the glacial Swamp Creek valley with yet more superb views, especially to Methow Pass, led to a long descent to the West Fork of the Methow River. The day ended with a steep 2,600 foot climb that climaxed with a set of very steep switchbacks that went straight up the canyon wall from Glacier Pass. Once the terrain eased off I searched for a camp site, finding one beside a tiny trickling creeklet amongst alpine larch and subalpine fir. Up here at 6,600 feet the air was chilly. A crescent moon appeared in the sky. I wasn't surprised to find a frost on the ground the next morning.

My penultimate day on the trail was another wonderful timberline walk through a spectacular landscape that took me into the huge (531,539 acres) and magnificent Pasayten Wilderness, (which I was to cross from east to west on the Pacific Northwest Trail many years later). The PCT stayed high on a traverse between several passes with views that included ones west to the vast array of peaks of the North Cascades National Park and beyond them the big white snow cone of Mount Baker. In this dry terrain there was a noticeable lack of creeks. The alpine larch I'd been enjoying the last few days gave way to subalpine fir and Engelmann spruce, tall spire-like conifers with short curved branches that shed snow easily. The autumn colours of red and yellow were vivid now, making the mountainsides beautiful and bright. Just once I dipped down into deeper forest to Holman Pass before climbing back up 1200 feet for my last wilderness camp by a barely flowing spring on a small flat area on the mountainside. I sat in the tent watching the trees and the sky and thinking about my long journey. I knew it had to end. I knew too that I wanted to do more walks like this. The satisfaction had been intense. The pleasure enormous. Some may concentrate on the heavy loads, difficult terrain and aching feet and think that long distance walking couldn't be really enjoyable. I couldn't imagine anything I could enjoy more. This, for me, was what life was all about. I thought back over the walk, back to the Mohave Desert and the heat, the High Sierra and the snow, Yosemite and the snowmelt creeks, marvellous Crater Lake, the endless rich forests, the beautiful mountains – Shasta, Jefferson,

Mount Hardy from Methow Pass

Camp in the Pasayten Wilderness

Autumn colours on the trail in the North Cascades
Trail sign near the US/Canada border

Glacier Peak –, the wildlife, the flowers, the narrow trail winding ever onwards through the wilderness, and shivered with delight. I would be back. On the trail anyway if not the PCT.

My hopes for a final spectacular day were dimmed when I woke to a cloudy sky. The sun did almost break through soon after dawn, turning the peaks across the valley a dark sombre red, but soon after I set off rain began to fall and a chill wind swept the mountains. I walked fast, not just with keenness to reach Canada, but also to keep warm. There were glimpses of rugged Three Fools Peak and down to pretty Hopkins Lake but mostly I saw nothing but dripping trees. I didn't feel disappointed though. How could I after what had gone before? At 12.45p.m. the trail, now in forest, opened out at a little clearing in which stood a stone obelisk, Monument 78. I had reached Canada. I had completed the PCT. The rain was torrential and the cloud was drifting through the trees. It was as unlike the beginning in the hot desert under a blue sky as was possible, which I felt was appropriate. I took some photos of my wet pack leaning against the monument. The pillar opened up and inside I found messages from other PCT hikers. I added a few comments of my own. Today there is a PCT monument here as well.

As the border is in the wilderness I still had 7 miles and 1000 feet of ascent to walk through the wet forest to Manning Provincial Park and the road that would take me away from the

177

The Finish! Monument 78 in the rain

PCT. Here I camped for the last time, on a wet campground noisy with the sound of traffic. I was no longer in the wilderness. At Monument 78 I'd felt elated and relieved. I'd made it! By Manning Park I felt numb and very sad. A highlight of my life was over. I was aware that the fact that I wouldn't hike the next day, that I had finished the PCT, hadn't really registered yet though and that it probably wouldn't until I was in Vancouver or even on the plane back to Britain. What I didn't know was that it never would register. In one sense I would never leave the PCT. It would always be with me and many times in the years to come I would recall events, landscapes, camps and more and suddenly be back there on that wonderful trail. I couldn't ask for more. But now it was time to go home.

THE PACIFIC CREST TRAIL
PRESENT AND FUTURE

Since 1982 the PCT in itself hasn't actually changed much. Only in the Mohave Desert and Tehachapi Mountains region is the route substantially different to the one I hiked. The terrain is much the same though. The day-to-day hiking experience hasn't changed either. You still have to carry everything you need. You still camp in the wilds far from roads and towns. You still move on every day. You still get dirty and sweaty. Your feet will hurt at times. So might your back. You will still have to deal with rain, snow, wind, sunshine. You will still have the immense joy of living in the wilderness week after week. You will still relish the comforts of trail towns, especially food.

In other ways the experience of hiking the PCT has changed enormously though, due in the main, I think, to two factors – popularity and the Internet- that are intertwined. The PCT was slowly growing in popularity in 1982 with some 120 thru-hiker permits issued and I did at times have a sense of a community on the move. But it was only a small community and mostly I was not aware of it at all. Now with 1000+ thru-hikers setting off every spring there really is a big PCT community on the move every year. You can hike the trail with others the whole way even if you set off solo if you're heading north. Southbounders, who are quite rare, are more likely to have an independent hike – most of the PCT hikers they meet will be heading in the other direction. For the northbound masses there's even an annual send-off party with the rather long-winded name of the Annual Zero Day Pacific Crest Trail Kick Off. This is held in late April every year at Lake Morena not far from the southern start of the trail. Here thru-hikers can find all the information they need, meet other hikers and enjoy films and gear stalls, presentations and seminars. Hikers can find up-to-date information on water sources in the desert and snow conditions in the mountains. They can get rides to the border too or to wherever they left the trail to attend the Kick Off. Of course all this is optional and hikers can skip the Kick Off and set off at a different time so they don't encounter many others if that's what they want. Or start at the Canadian Border. Most thru-hikers do go to the Kick Off even if they've already begun the trail. For many hikers meeting others and sharing the trail is a major part of the experience. Reading some recent accounts and talking to some recent thru-hikers can make the PCT sound like a moving party with an emphasis on people, beer, towns, rides and food rather than on the landscape or the wildlife. I'm pleased so many people enjoy the PCT now but in many ways I'm glad I did the trail when it was quieter.

The early pioneers of the trail – Martin Papendick, Eric Ryback, Teddi Boston – weren't concerned about how long the hike took. They were just intent on completing a thru-hike, a massive challenge in itself. The same applied to me and other hikers in the 1980s. Five and a half to six months was accepted as the time required. That began to change in 1991 when Ray and Jenny Jardine hiked the PCT in 3 months and 3 days. How they did this is explained in Ray's *The Pacific Crest Trail Hiker's Handbook*, which also included itineraries for thru-hikes of different lengths, the first ever published. This led to interest in how fast the trail could be hiked and setting a record time became a challenge for some hikers. The current records for unsupported (traditional thru-hiker style) and supported (with a backup crew) were set in 2013 and 2014. Heather 'Anish' Anderson's 2013 unsupported hike took 60 days, 17 hours and 12 minutes. She averaged nearly 44 miles a day. A year later Joe McConaughy completed an supported hike in 53 days, 6 hours and 37 minutes, an average of 50 miles a day. These are astonishing achievements. By comparison my hike took 174 days and I averaged about 15 miles a day. I wasn't setting out to do a fast hike of course. Nor would I want to even try but I do have great admiration for those who do.

Others set out to do two thru-hikes back-to-back, known as a yo-yo hike, by simply turning round at the Canadian border and heading back to Mexico. The first to achieve this was Scott Williamson in 2004. The double PCT hike took him 197 days and he averaged 27 miles a day. Two years later he repeated the feat in 191 days. Williamson also held the record for the fastest PCT hike for many years and has thru-hiked the PCT thirteen times.

In the future others will set out to break the speed record and the yo-yo record. Someone may even attempt a triple PCT hike. Most hikers though will still take around 4-5 months. And many won't finish. The PCTA estimates maybe 50% don't complete the trail. That's lower than in the past, undoubtedly due to better information and equipment (lighter weight in particular) being available.

The popularity of the trail had its first big surge back in the 1970s with the publication of Eric Ryback's book *The High Adventure of Eric Ryback*, which attracted much media attention. In 2012 another book led to increased interest in the trail – Cheryl Strayed's *Wild: From Lost to Found on the Pacific Crest Trail*, which has sold over a million copies. *Wild* was picked for Oprah's Book Club and had masses of coverage in the media worldwide – it was broadcast as Book of the Week on BBC Radio 4 in 2013. Strayed didn't hike the whole trail but she did hike enough of it – some 1100 miles – to convey much of what it's like to be a thru-hiker. The book tells the story of how she found herself and recovered from a very bad personal situation by hiking the trail, a story that has inspired many non-hikers to try the trail or parts of it themselves. A year after the book was published over 1000 applications for through-hike permits were made for the first time.

Wild is now being made into a Hollywood movie starring Reese Witherspoon with a screenplay by Nick Hornby. It's due to be released in late 2014. This will give the PCT massively more coverage than it has ever had before and is likely to lead to a huge increase in would-be thru-hikers from 2015 onwards. Many, I suspect, will be hoping the trail will have the same life-changing effect it had on Cheryl Strayed. If so, I hope it does.

Is this increased popularity good or bad for the trail? Some hikers certainly feel a quieter trail would be preferable and also worry that increased popularity will mean more novices setting out who aren't really experienced enough for the trail. I don't agree. Simply by setting off at a different time to most hikers or hiking southbound it is still possible to have a fairly solitary hike. Novices will either learn quickly or abandon the trail. I was a complete novice at desert hiking at the start, as shown by mistakes with footwear and how much water to carry. I was a novice at long-distance hiking through snowbound mountains too and had never used snowshoes before. I learnt much on the trail. I also think there is one big reason to welcome the growing popularity of the PCT and that is that it leads to a greater constituency of people who want to protect the trail and the landscape it passes through. The more people who love the trail, the more people there are who feel a connection with the PCT, with the Mohave Desert, the High Sierra and the Cascades; the more people there are to stand up and shout when these landscapes are threatened. I'm also in favour of encouraging people to venture into wild places and take up hiking and backpacking for reasons of health and well-being. Hiking is good for you! You don't need to be in the dismal position Cheryl Strayed was in to gain much from hiking the PCT.

More people is good for the places along the trail too. Many had never heard of the PCT in 1982 and the smaller ones often had few facilities or supplies suitable for hikers. Now with many hundreds of people passing through each year places set out to welcome hikers and have everything they need. This is of mutual benefit to businesses and hikers alike. Camp sites and hiker accommodation, trail food and gear, shuttles to and from trailheads, hiker boxes for unwanted gear are all available in various places.

The network of trail angels was just beginning to develop back when I hiked the PCT. Now with the growing popularity of the PCT there are trail angels all along the trail who help hikers with lifts, accommodation, supplies, meals and more. Some put out water caches in dry areas. Some wait at road crossings to give hikers lifts to towns. Many hikers find their trips easier because of unselfish help from trail angels. There are other volunteers who work on maintaining the trail and keeping it in good condition. They are less seen by hikers than those who provide assistance along the way but they are just as valuable. I think they are trail angels too.

Another feature of PCT hiking that has arrived with its growing popularity is trail names. Most hikers now have a trail name, bestowed on them by other hikers. These can be descriptive, humorous or frankly bizarre. A selection from the 2013 hikers list on the PCTA website includes Reason, Miracle Zen, Kindergarten Cop, Oatmeal, Old Goat, Fun Size, Treekiller, The Viking and Sharkbite. I've never had a trail name as I've never done a trail popular enough at the time for these to have been used. One day maybe!

With popularity has come more information, making planning a thru-hike much easier than it was in 1982. The Internet has made accessing and disseminating this information fast and simple. Indeed, the problem today is likely to be too much information rather than too little. The key organisation here is the Pacific Crest Trail Association whose website has a wealth of information about every aspect of the PCT from thru-hiking to trail maintenance to conservation. Up-to-date information is available on everything from facilities in towns to conditions on the trail. And if the information you require isn't there you can ask online. Often replies will come in very quickly.

Whilst the PCTA provides important information for hikers there are other sources, particularly the American Long Distance Hiking Association – West. ALDHA-West is not just about the PCT but the trail is central to it. Every autumn ALDHA-West holds a Gathering with talks, discussions and videos by long distance hikers, many of them that year's PCT completers. I've attended a couple of these Gatherings and they are very energising and inspiring.

The Internet can also provide route descriptions and data that can be downloaded to a smartphone or GPS unit. You can hike the PCT with all the information you need on a tiny electronic device (though I would advise combining it with paper maps and guides too). Traditional publishing hasn't disappeared though. Updated versions of the Wilderness Press guidebooks I used are still available and still used by most hikers (and still torn into sections and posted ahead), backed up by books such as *Yogi's Pacific Crest Trail Handbook* that contain all the information needed for planning and logistics. There are excellent maps, such as Halfmile's, showing the whole of the trail and with much more detail than the strip maps from the Pacific Crest Club I used. Many accounts of hiking the trail have now been published too so it's easier to get a feel for the experience without setting foot on the PCT. I've listed a few that I've read and enjoyed in the bibliography. I could have planned my PCT hike in a tenth of the time with all this material and had far more details about the trail as well. Whilst I'm happy to have hiked the trail before planning was so easy it does open up the trail to more people. And however much information you have walking the PCT hasn't changed. The desert is still hot. The mountains are still steep. The mosquitoes still bite. The rain still falls. Hiking the PCT is never going to be easy. But the rewards will always be great.

The Internet, GPS and digital technology have also changed the ways in which hikers can share their experience and stay in touch with friends and family. For much of my hike no-one knew where I was. By the time the postcards I sent home or the reports I sent to Warren Rogers arrived I was many days further along the trail. Today hikers can send daily satellite signals giving their position or even, if they have enough battery power, transmit the route of their hike as they go along. The same devices can be used to call for help in case of an emergency. In the High Sierra Scott, Dave, Larry and I were usually several days away from any help and we would have had to hike out to find it. Today help could arrive in hours. This makes the trail safer but does have risks. Technology may not always work. Sometimes a signal may not get through. Sometimes you may not be in a position to send one. Having the skills to deal with the wilderness and always taking care are still essential. You can't rely on gadgets to get you out of trouble.

I shared my PCT experience with a couple of reports in the Pacific Crest Club Quarterly during my hike and then an article in a British hiking magazine afterwards. Only a small number of people will have seen these. Today many hikers upload their journals and photos to the Internet during their hike. The PCTA keeps a list of these journals with links on its website and you can also find them on the Trail Journals website. As well as following current hikers these sites host journals from the past, a fascinating archive.

Uploading photos to social media sites, blogs and trail journals was beyond imagination in 1982. Digital photography did not exist. Everything was film. I used transparency film as this is what editors liked for publication and which I could use for illustrated talks and slide shows (a name still often used for digital presentations). The film was Kodachrome 64, the figure indicating the ISO speed. One roll of 36 shots weighed an ounce so I didn't carry dozens of rolls and had to ration shots. There are many photos I would have taken with a digital camera that I didn't because of this. I really wish I'd carried more film now but I wouldn't have wanted the extra weight at the time. Of course I couldn't see the results until after the walk and I often worried about films being lost in the post. I sent them for development in small bundles with the hope that most would get through. In fact none disappeared. For recording a thru-hike I think digital photography has been a major breakthrough. Now you can photograph everything of interest. Digital cameras are small and lightweight and with the quality of phone cameras rising all the time it may soon be unnecessary to carry a standalone camera at all. And whenever you have an Internet connection you can upload an image, sometimes from seemingly remote places (though of course along much of the PCT there won't be an Internet connection).

Also significant has been the so-called 'lightweight revolution' in outdoor gear, sparked in part by Ray and Jenny Jardine's PCT experiences, resulting in *The Pacific Crest Trail Hiker's Handbook* (the ideas of which are continued in Ray Jardine's current book *Trail Life*), and also by the development of lighter, stronger materials for backpacking equipment. Hikers can now carry much lighter gear than I did and have the same comfort and security. What constituted 'lightweight' in 1982 is very different from today. Many now standard modern materials – titanium, silnylon, fleece, microfibers, cuben fibre – just didn't exist back then. If I did the PCT now my pack would be much lighter. Everything from ice axe to tent to the pack itself would weigh less. I'd still have carried a big load through the High Sierra – food isn't any lighter – but it wouldn't have been so ridiculously horrendous.

Beyond all these changes in communications and equipment, beyond books and films and journals, beyond the mass of information the Pacific Crest Trail lies waiting. The reasons for going – the beauty and challenge of the wilderness – have not changed. The desert is still the same, still as hot, as dry, as strange. The mountains are still the same too. The passes of the High Sierra are still steep, rocky and rough. The landscape is still glorious. The forests are still magnificent. Bald eagles still soar over the mountains. Bears still prowl the woods. The PCT is magnificent. It's worth going to have a look.

BIBLIOGRAPHY

BOOKS

Arno, Stephen *Northwest Trees: Identifying and Understanding the Region's Native Trees*, The Mountaineers, 2007

Beckey, Fred *The Challenge of the North Cascades*, The Mountaineers, 1996

Berger, Karen and Smith, Daniel R, *The Pacific Crest Trail: A Hiker's Companion*, Countryman Press, 2014

Bull, John and Farrand, John (Editors), *The Audubon Society Field Guide to North American Birds: Western Region*, Random House, 1988

Clarke, Clinton C. *The Pacific Crest Trailway*, 1945, available online at pcttrailway.pctplanner.com

Fletcher, Colin *The Thousand-Mile Summer in Desert and High Sierra*, Vintage, 1989

Foskett, Keith *The Last Englishman: A 2,650 Mile Hiking Adventure on the Pacific Crest Trail*, CreateSpace, 2012

Go, Benedict *Pacific Crest Trail Data Book*, Wilderness Press, 2013

Green, David *A Pacific Crest Odyssey: Walking the Trail from Mexico to Canada*, Wilderness Press, 1979

Harris, Stephen L. *Fire Mountains of the West: The Cascade And Mono Lake Volcanoes*, Mountain Press, 2005

Hughes, Rees & Lewis, Corey *The Pacific Crest Trailside Reader: California*, The Mountaineers, 2011

Hughes, Rees & Lewis, Corey *The Pacific Crest Trailside Reader: Oregon & Washington*, The Mountaineers, 2011

Jardine, Ray *The Pacific Crest Trail Hiker's Handbook*, AdventureLore Press, 1996

Jardine, Ray *Trail Life*, AdventureLore Press, 2009

Johnson, Brian *The Pacific Crest Trail (A Cicerone Guide)*, Cicerone Press, 2010

Kerouac, Jack *The Dharma Bums* Penguin Modern Classics, 2007

Lindsay, Ann and House, Syd *The Tree Collector: The Life and Explorations of David Douglas,* Aurum, 2005

Long, Chuck *Pacific Crest Trail Hike Planning Guide*, Signpost, 1976

McDonnell, Jackie *Yogi's Pacific Crest Trail Handbook,* Yogi's Books, 2014

Moore, James G. *Exploring the Highest Sierra*, Stanford University Press, 2002

Muir, John *The Eight Wilderness-Discovery Books*, Diadem, 1992

Nisbet, Jack *The Collector: David Douglas and the Natural History of the Northwest*, Sasquatch Books, 2009

Nisbet, Jack *Sources of the River: Tracking David Thompson Across Western North America*, Sasquatch Books, 2007

Ross, Cindy *Journey on the Crest: Walking 2600 Miles from Mexico to Canada*, The Mountaineers, 1987

Ryback, Eric *The High Adventure of Eric Ryback*, Bantam, 1973

Schaffer, Jeffrey P. and Selters, Andy *Pacific Crest Trail: Oregon and Washington*, Wilderness Press, 2004

Schaffer, Jeffrey P. *Pacific Crest Trail: Northern California*, Wilderness Press, 2003

Schirfin, Ben; Schaffer, Jeffrey P; Winnett, Thomas and Jenkins, Ruby Johnson *Pacific Crest Trail: Southern California*, Wilderness Press, 2003

Snyder, Gary *A Range of Poems*, Fulcrum, 1967

Strayed, Cheryl *Wild: From Lost to Found on the Pacific Crest Trail*, Vintage, 2013

Townsend, Chris *Grizzly Bears and Razor Clams: Walking America's Pacific Northwest Trail*, Sandstone Press, 2012

Townsend, Chris *The Backpacker's Handbook*, McGraw-Hill, Fourth Edition 2011

Walker, Bill *Skywalker: Highs and Lows on the Pacific Crest Trail*, CreateSpace, 2010

Watts, Tom *Pacific Coast Tree Finder*, Wilderness Press, 2004

Whitney, Stephen *A Sierra Club Naturalist's Guide to The Sierra Nevada*, Sierra Club Books, 1982

Whitney, Stephen R & Sandelin, Rob *A Field Guide to the Cascades & Olympics*, The Mountaineers, 2004

DVD

Tell It On The Mountain – Tales from the Pacific Crest Trail directed by Lisa Diener

WEBSITES

Pacific Crest Trail Association www.pcta.org

American Long Distance Hiking Association – West www.aldhawest.org

Annual Day Zero Pacific Crest Trail Kick Off www.adzpctko.org

Trail Journals www.trailjournals.com/journals/pacific_crest_trail/

Yogi's Books www.yogisbooks.com